42 Days to Feeling Great

BOB PHILLIPS

HARVEST HOUSE PUBLISHERS

Eugene, Oregon 97402

Cover by Left Coast Design, Portland, Oregon

42 DAYS TO FEELING GREAT

Copyright © 2001 by Bob Phillips
Published by Harvest House Publishers
Eugene, Oregon 97402

Library of Congress Cataloging-in-Publication Data
Phillips, Bob, 1940–
    42 days to feeling great! / Bob Phillips
        p. cm.
    ISBN 0-7369-0379-8
        1. Emotions—Religious aspects—Christianity.   2. Christianity—Psychology.   I. Title:
    Forty-two days to feeling great. II. Title.
    BV4597.3.P48 2001
    248.4—dc21   00-054183

Printed in the United States of America

01 02 03 04 05 06 07 / RDP-CF/ 10 9 8 7 6 5 4 3 2 1

To Charles "Tremendous" Jones,
a man who has dedicated his life
to helping people know God,
grow in their personal lives,
and give their lives in
service to others.

Contents

Before You Begin Your Journey

Begin to weave and God will give the thread.

THE FOG WAS THICK AND A CHILLY breeze cut through the warmest of coats. Even those who had lived in London for most of their lives couldn't remember such a cold day. It was amazing to see so many people making their way through the early nineteenth-century London streets on such a dreary day. One man emerged from the crowd and entered a doorway. The sign above it read: *Physician's Office.*

In the presence of the doctor, the man shared how depressed and dejected he had been feeling for some months. He opened his heart and confessed that he had been contemplating suicide.

After hearing the man's story the doctor responded. "You need to be cheered up. You need some laughter. You need to go to the entertainment heart of London.

7

> You need to go down to Piccadilly Circus where the
> world famous clown Grimaldi is making everyone
> smile. He will cheer you up and make you feel better."

> The man responded, "I am Grimaldi the Clown!"

Have you ever wondered if it's really possible to change your emotions? Have you been feeling like Grimaldi the Clown? Just moving through life making everyone else laugh and feel good while you are dying inside? If so, I've got good news for you! You can change those bad feelings into great feelings in 42 days.

Everyone experiences grief, hurt, and loss. As a result, our tangled and knotted emotions sometime overpower our thinking process. We begin to feel bad, mad, or sad. Many counselors believe the majority of life's problems are rooted in broken and damaged relationships. Others think most of our difficulties are tied to feelings of low self-esteem. No one book can address all the specific problems in life. You would need a whole library to do that. *42 Days to Feeling Great* was written to challenge your thinking with regard to three basic questions:

1. What is going on?
2. How do you feel about it?
3. Do you want to change?

Together, we'll consider seven important principles that can help you change how you're feeling:

1. People only change when they hurt enough.
2. Making peace with pain is the way to healing.
3. Being honest is the starting place for growth.
4. Dealing with anger changes your thinking.

5. Forgiveness can become the road to health.

6. Giving to others makes us mature.

7. Finding our purpose gives us motivation.

It takes about six weeks (42 days) to make lasting changes to habit patterns. The three questions and seven principles just mentioned provide a launching pad or starting point for change. They are written to challenge your thinking and spur your attitude to change from the negative to the positive. They will also encourage you to not give up during the 42 days of habit-pattern changes in your life.

You come from a unique background and face your own set of circumstances and problems. You may have negative habits you would like to get rid of or positive habits you'd like to establish. Maybe you have relationships that need to be worked on. Do you need to exercise forgiveness to others or yourself? If you follow through on the questions and principles in this book, you *will* experience hope and peace. If, after finishing this book, you undertake what is suggested, I am confident you will be feeling great.

They sailed. They sailed. Then spake the mate:
"This mad sea shows its teeth tonight.
He curls his lip, he lies in wait,
With lifted teeth, as if to bite!
Brave Admiral, say but one good word:
What shall we do when hope is gone?"
The words leapt like a leaping sword:
"Sail on! sail on! sail on! and on!"

Joaquin Miller

What Is Going On?

Life is like an onion: you peel it off one layer at a time, and sometimes you weep.

Carl Sandburg

I BEGAN RUNNING AS FAST AS I COULD, yet it felt as if everything around me was in slow motion. I tried to yell but no sound would come. I could feel the panic as the beast drew closer and closer. I knew that this time my life would end." Bill was describing a recurring nightmare that had become an obsession. "That dream has bothered me for years," he continued. "But, recently, something far worse has taken its place. This new monster is larger and ten times more scary than the beast of my nightmares. Not only do I battle it during the night, I now struggle with it during the day."

I could see the agitation in Bill's face as he sat forward in his chair. "You see it all started about a month ago when I brought home the new computer. I had hooked up with an Internet provider and was 'surfing the Web' when something popped on the screen. Out of curiosity, I clicked on the advertisement and up came a pornography site. I thought to myself, 'I've heard about these sites. I wonder what all the fuss is about.' At first, I only looked at a few pictures and then shut it down. I knew this was not the best thing for me to be doing. When I went to bed that night I could not get those pictures out of my mind."

Bill leaned back in the chair and gazed out the window for a moment. The silence seemed to last a long time. As he turned back, I could hear the anguish in his voice. "I'm hooked. I know that I'm addicted. I can't stop looking at those pictures. It is a monster I can't get away from. I think about it all day long at work. How can I kill this beast?"

ROSE CAME IN THE ROOM with a big smile on her face. In one hand she was carrying her purse and in the other a large shopping sack. She placed the sack on the floor and sat down on the couch. She began to tell me what a great day of shopping she had at the mall. Soon the mall story was giving way to deeper issues and concerns.

"I know I should be happy, but I'm not. I have a wonderful husband, three great kids, and a beautiful home. Yet every time I look at myself in the mirror I want to throw up. I have gained so much weight after having Roger, and I just can't get rid of it. I think I have tried every diet plan on the market. I don't seem to have any willpower. I'm doomed to carry all this blubber around with me for the rest of my life."

Rose's big smile had turned to tears of pain and frustration.

IT WAS AFTER CHURCH IN THE HALLWAY when Sally touched my arm. As I turned, she said, "Do you have a moment that I could talk to you?" We stepped to the side of the hall to let other people go by and she started with hesitation.

"Could I come in and see you next week?"

"Of course," I said.

"I need to talk to someone. I think I am going crazy. I feel like everyone runs over me. I can't say no to anyone. I hate any kind of confrontation or people being upset with me. I just hold my feelings inside. I have a low self-image, and I know I'm a loser. I've stopped going to social events. I just want to run away from all the stress I'm feeling. I have even had thoughts that life is just not worth living."

It was easy to tell that Sally was under a great deal of turmoil. She poured out her pain in a few short moments of time.

BILL, ROSE, AND SALLY were not feeling great. In fact, they were feeling just the opposite. They were hurting.

We live in a stress-producing society that spends billions of dollars each year dealing with mental-health issues. Depression has become a growing, universal experience in our country, and suicide is a major cause of death. Those attempting to cope with nervous breakdowns, stress disorders, and emotional exhaustion consume carloads of aspirin, painkillers, and sleeping medications.

There are many causes or reasons why people do not feel good emotionally: life events over which they have no control, losing loved ones through accidents or illnesses, and losing jobs and financial support. Personal illnesses or accidents disrupt entire families. Catastrophic disasters like fires, floods, earthquakes, or tornados devastate finances and personal property. People also struggle with minor negative habits they would like to have victory over. These habits may not be terrible in and of themselves, but they are a cause of constant irritation to the person with the habit and those around him or her. Can you identify with any of the habits listed below?

Being late	Hair twisting
Belching	Jaw clenching
Chronic forgetfulness	Nail biting
Cracking knuckles	Obsessive orderliness
Fidgeting	Passing gas
Finger tapping	Sloppiness
Gum snapping	Toe tapping

Habit is a habit and not to be flung out of the window by any man but coaxed downstairs a step at a time.

Mark Twain

There are some individuals that develop irrational and unwarranted fears that are commonly called phobias. Even though people may be aware that the fears are groundless, they still struggle with ridding themselves of that fear. Listed below are some of the more common phobias.

Acrophobia	Fear of high places
Agoraphobia	Fear of open places
Aichmophobia	Fear of sharp or pointed objects
Algophobia	Fear of pain
Anthropophobia	Fear of men or of a particular man
Astraphobia	Fear of thunder, lightning, or storms

Claustrophobia	Fear of closed places
Ereutophobia	Fear of blushing
Gynophobia	Fear of women or of a particular woman
Hematophobia	Fear of blood
Hydrophobia	Fear of water
Monophobia	Fear of solitude
Necrophobia	Fear of dead bodies
Nyctophobia	Fear of darkness (night)
Ochlophobia	Fear of crowds
Pathophobia	Fear of disease or some particular disease
Pyrophobia	Fear of fire or causing fire
Thanatophobia	Fear of death
Toxophobia	Fear of poisons or being poisoned
Zoophobia	Fear of animals or some particular animal

Along with phobias, some individuals develop "obsessions" and "compulsions." An obsession takes the form of a repetitive and uncontrollable thought. People are unable to shake off their thoughts. They might take the form of self-accusatory put-downs, such as: "I'm no good," "I can't do anything right," "I always make a fool of myself." Often the people think they are losing their minds. Sometimes they continually think of antisocial acts or vulgar thoughts. They might be filled with insistent doubts about their own functioning, other people's love for them, or how God could possibly love them because they are too bad and sinful.

People filled with obsessions often have a difficult time making decisions. They do not trust their own memory. They always double and triple check to see if the door is locked, the lights are turned out, and the iron is unplugged. Sometimes they will reopen the envelopes they have just sealed for reassurance that everything was included and filled out correctly. These obsessive behaviors drain energy. They hamper mental health and may even affect physical health. Usually obsessive behaviors are associated with some type of guilt feelings or unworthiness. Often they are tied to the fact that the person came from a home where the parents were punitive, prohibiting, and unforgiving.

Compulsions are similar to obsessions in that the individuals have repetitive, meaningless urges. These usually are displayed in trivial behaviors that take on a ritualistic character. For example, when I was a child I was told that if I stepped on a crack in the sidewalk it would harm my mother: "Don't step on a crack or you'll break your mother's back." We can now smile at this ridiculous thought and even laugh at children as they hop over cracks in the sidewalk. But if someone is 30 years of age and still stepping over cracks, what was a childish game has become a compulsion. Compulsive behaviors include picking up things on the sidewalk or touching every other lamppost.

People with compulsions are feeling an anxiety they usually can't define. They believe that by following a particular ritual they will feel better. However, these rituals only give temporary pleasure or relief. Because of this, compulsive people often intensify their ritualistic behaviors in the hope of finding some type of lasting emotional relief.

We think it is cute when a baby cannot go to sleep without its special blanket. But it is not funny or cute when adults must go through a ritual of touching certain things in the house before they go to bed. Often persons with compulsions have little "magical" phrases or incantations they repeat, they snap their fingers, or count certain numbers. They may have a ritual of washing their hands and drying them in a particular manner. Sometimes when they are driving down the street they will say to themselves, "If the light turns green, I will buy an ice cream cone. If it turns red, I will abstain."

To help clarify the difference between obsessions and compulsions, remember: An obsession is usually a mental process; a compulsion is a physical process. The first involves thinking more, and the second involves acting more.

With an obsession, the individual has an idea or a series of ideas that frequently and tenaciously reoccur. The preoccupation with these fixed ideas, or unwanted feelings, often interferes with the normal thinking process. The idividual feels mentally harassed by these thoughts.

For example, an obsessive person might become anxious and worry a great deal about being physically attacked in public. These thoughts of possibly being hurt begin to overwhelm them. They envision people breaking into their homes, being beaten up by a hoodlum, or becoming involved in a carjacking. These thoughts continue to preoccupy their minds throughout the day and night regardless if they are based on reality or simply imagined. They begin to live their lives in mental fear.

**Habits are first cobwebs,
then cables.**

A compulsion on the other hand is an irresistible impulse to perform an act in some way regardless of the rationality or motivation. This reaction may even be contrary to one's better judgment. The physical act of doing something, temporarily releases some of the inner tension the individual is feeling. It seems to help reduce the anxiety for the moment by doing the activity or ritual.

For example: the same person who is afraid of being physically attacked might compulsively carry a cane or umbrella to ward off an attacker. They might also carry a can of mace to spray in the face of the attacker. The compulsive person would never go out in public without protective devices. They would be constantly looking around to see who was going to attack them. Their inner fears would be carried out in protective behaviors that would go far beyond the average person.

It would be impossible to include every emotion or event that creates negative feelings, anxiety, or mental stress in life. The following is a list of the most common issues, behaviors, thoughts, and feelings that generate negative emotions. Place a check by the ones you are dealing with or experiencing at this time in your life.

Alcoholism	Cowardice	Feeling weak
Anger	Critical	Feeling worthless
Anxiety	Death	Fighting
Bitterness	Deceitfulness	Gambling
Blaming	Depression	Gossiping
Boasting	Disappointment	Greed
Boredom	Discontent	Grief
Bossiness	Disillusionment	Guilt
Causing dissention	Divorce	Hatred
Change	Drugs	Heading nowhere
Cheating	Emotional exhaustion	Health issues
Complaining	Envy	Homosexuality
Conceit	Excuse making	Ignored
Confinement	Fear	Impatient
Confusion	Fear of failure	Imperfection
Contaminated	Fear of intimacy	Impulsive
Covetousness	Feeling stupid	Impure thoughts
		Insecure

Instability	Overly quiet	Self-hatred
Isolation	Overly sensitive	Self-indulgent
Jealousy	Panic	Self-pity
Job change	Paralysis	Self-sufficient
Lazy	Perfectionism	Sense of failure
Left out	Pornography	Sensuality
Loneliness	Prejudice	Sexual addiction
Loser mentality	Pride	Sexual lust
Losing control	Procrastination	Shoplifting
Loss	Profanity	Shyness
Loss of dream	Promise breaker	Smoking
Low self-image	Rebellion	Stealing
Lying	Regret	Stubbornness
Masturbation	Rejection	Temper tantrums
Midlife crisis	Resentment	Tension
Moving	Resistance	Thrill seeking
Negative thinking	Restlessness	Turmoil
Not finishing projects	Risk taking	Unforgiveness
Obsessional thinking	Sadness	Unloved
	Scared	Unspoken expectations
Occult involvement	Self-centeredness	
	Self-deprecation	Vandalism
Overeating	Self-gratification	Vanity

Is it possible to eliminate or at least change some of these negative feelings? The answer is yes. You *can* feel great *if you want to*. That is what this book is all about. To reach that point, three questions must be answered:

1. What is going on?
2. How do you feel about it?
3. Do you want to change?

In this chapter we looked at the various emotions and events that cause us to feel badly. Did any of them ring bells with you? Did you put a check by the ones you may be struggling with? The first step in the process to feeling great is to identify where you are emotionally. You see, life is a journey. Some of the paths lead down beautiful garden walkways and others beside the garbage dump and the sewer pond. Life is not perfect or predictable. Our job is to keep walking forward instead of taking detours through the ruts of negative emotions and the washouts of misery.

This does not mean that we can avoid hurt, loss, and pain. They are part of the human experience. These three great teachers force us into the arms of God. If we don't run from them, we will grow and learn from them.

Have you been struggling through the zone of discontentment? Have you been trying to discover the meaning of your present circumstances? Don't lose heart; don't give up. All of nature teaches us that there are seasons to life. We all have to go through falls and winters before we can enjoy springs and summers.

During the winter, the ground is fallow and nothing seems to grow. There is only barrenness. It seems as if everything has come to an end. Life is filled with "endings." Grade school ends. Junior high school ends. High school and college end. We move to another state to start a new job and end work and social relationships we have known for years. Sometimes endings take the forms of divorce or separation.

Most endings begin with something going wrong; a hurtful or painful experience transpires. We wish we could escape but we can't. Parents and friends die, and we will experience our own endings. Many other endings also have the smell and taste of death. Even though we know the reality and finality of death in any form, we still try to avoid it. No one is alone with that emotion.

**If finding God's way in the suddenness
of storms makes our faith grow broad,
then trusting God's wisdom in the
[dailyness] of living makes it grow deep.
And strong. Whatever may be your
circumstances—however long it may have
lasted—wherever you may be today,
I bring this reminder: The stronger the
winds, the deeper the roots, and the longer
the winds...the more beautiful the tree.**

Chuck Swindoll

Endings must occur before there can be beginnings. The ending you are experiencing is really a new beginning...if you will only recognize and embrace it. Everyone faces problems and difficulties. No magical form of thinking "What if" will remove the reality and truth of what you are going through. Recognize where you are now in this journey and where you would like to be in the days ahead. God will lead you there if you put your trust in Him.

Taking Action

1. Are you ready to step onto the stage and play your part?

2. What "script" have you been following?

3. What would you like your new role to be?

4. List the negative habits you would like to overcome, the attitudes you would like to change, and the emotions you would like to eliminate.

5. Are there any damaged relationships you would like to see healed? (Be specific.)

> And I am sure that God who began the good work within you will keep right on helping you grow in his grace until his task within you is finally finished on that day when Jesus Christ returns (Philippians 1:6).

How Do You
Feel About It?

2

> *By starving emotions we become humorless,*
> *rigid and stereotyped; by repressing them we*
> *become literal, reformatory and holier-than-*
> *thou; encouraged, they perfume life; discour-*
> *aged, they poison it.*
>
> Joseph Collins

I JUST CAN'T BELIEVE THAT MY MOTHER would not come to my daughter's birthday party. She said it was because I didn't call her last week. Ever since dad died, she has become more and more difficult to get along with. If you don't do something her way or meet her expectations, she tries to punish you by holding back her love or involvement. It's so childish." Kim spent half an hour describing the relationship with her mother. She expressed frustration and anger over her mother's demanding and immature behavior. This was not the first time Kim had to deal with the issues of manipulation and withholding affection. During most of her childhood her mother had acted this way.

Kim is experiencing deep hurt. The *emotion of hurt* comes when there is a loss or injury. When hurt is not expressed, it leaves the pain inside. When someone is hurt they feel victimized, cheated, used, disappointed, overwhelmed, sorrowful, and frustrated. It is very important to discover what loss means to you. It is the first step in overcoming the pain of hurt. A good question to ask yourself when you feel the pain of hurt is, "What have I lost?"

BRIAN WAS DOWNRIGHT ANGRY. "I've worked my tail off for that stupid company for 23 years. Now they say they want someone younger to do my job. They want to give me the 'golden handshake,' a watch, and say goodbye. It's not fair!"

Anger involves pain that is expressed regardless of the time that has elapsed since the event. Anger carries with it the desire to strike out in some way. Those who experience this strong emotion are irritated, annoyed, furious, resentful, and bitter.

Much of whether we have a happy life or an unhappy life is determined by coming to terms with pain.

DIANA SHOULD HAVE BEEN very excited and happy. Her wedding was only 45 days away. But she was far from happy. In fact, she was in tears as her story unfolded. "I feel so terrible. I just can't get it out of my mind. It happened when I was a junior in high school. This boy and I had sex at his house when his parents weren't home. I didn't get pregnant or anything, but I think it is unfair to my fiancé. I feel so guilty."

Guilt usually comes about as a result of past pain that has not been expressed. It involves anger that is held in. The anger is usually directed inward. People are angry that they were so stupid...angry that the situation cannot be changed or forgotten. Guilt, whether real or false, makes someone feel unworthy, self-hating, self-blaming, remorseful, ashamed, and basically like he or she is just a bad person.

CARL WAS VERY QUIET. He didn't seem to want to talk. He gave short responses to my questions and sighed a lot. It took quite a bit of time before he began to open up.

"I've lost almost everything I've made during the last 13 years. I can't believe that Steve would do this to me. We've known each other since high school. We went to college together and then went into partnership in our office supply business. Steve basically did the books and the behind-the-scenes activities, while I was out front with sales and meeting customers. About six months ago, Steve abruptly left his wife and moved to another state. I know there was another woman involved. But the kicker for me is that he left with all of the money we had in the bank, and the creditors are yelling their heads off. I have no idea where he is. I am ruined."

Carl was visibly depressed. *Depression comes about when past pain, hurt, loss, and anger are not expressed.* The individuals hold in all of these emotions. This holding-in process depletes people of their energy. They feel lifeless, listless, blue, melancholy, despairing, and hopeless. One of the greatest hurts comes when someone has been dishonest with us.

AMANDA WAS VISIBLY AGITATED. Her nervousness was displayed by the constant twisting of the handkerchief that was in her hands. She began by saying, "This week I have to take the SAT exam for my teaching credential and I'm scared. I've studied hard but I don't think I'm going to pass."

Amanda was filled with anxiety. The emotion of *anxiety is the future expectation of some hurt or loss.* It is the awful feeling that something bad is going to happen. It expresses itself with feelings of worry, insecurity, helplessness, fearfulness, and uncertainty. The person becomes uptight, edgy, jittery, and experiences "cold feet."

ANGER, GUILT, DEPRESSION, ANXIETY. Feelings are a gauge of what we have been thinking about or how we perceive things. If we have been thinking positive, healthy thoughts, we will have correspondingly happy feelings. Conversely, if we have been entertaining negative, unhealthy thoughts, we will have bad feelings. *Thinking determines feeling.* Our "feeling gauge" registers either pain or pleasure. Feelings of pleasure help to increase our emotional energy level. Feelings of pain drain our emotional batteries, and our minds rally to this threat with defense mechanisms to protect our emotional well-being.

It has been estimated that the average person has approximately 50,000 thoughts enter and leave their mind every day. *(No wonder I'm so tired!)* Although we do not always have control over the thoughts that enter our minds, we do have control over whether we entertain them or not. The great reformer Martin Luther expressed this concept when he spoke of troublesome thoughts: "We cannot stop the birds from flying over our heads, but we can stop them from building a nest in our hair."

When we assume responsibility for our thinking, we assume responsibility for our feelings. When we assume responsibility for our feelings, we assume responsibility for our emotional health. The quality of our mental health is directly related to our thinking patterns. Dr. Richard Carlson stated it this way: "Happy people are able to see their thoughts as thoughts and dismiss the ones they don't want."

Have you learned how to dismiss unwanted thoughts? Or do you see yourself as a victim of your thoughts, ever held in their firm grip? Dr. Carlson goes on to say, "Being upset by your own thoughts is similar to writing yourself a nasty letter—and then being offended by that letter." Remember, you have the power to control your thoughts. How about trying a little experiment to illustrate the concept of changing your thoughts?

First, remember a painful experience out of your child-hood. It may have been a time when you were late, or wet your pants, or were embarrassed in front of a group of your peers. Just pause for a moment, put down this book, and think about that painful time. If I were sitting in front of you, would you be able to describe where you were, what time of day it was, and who was there?

I'll bet if you thought about this event long enough you could even feel the same emotions you felt when it occurred. If you continued thinking about the hurt, pain, and loss, it would begin to grow. With enough focus and thought, you might even increase the suffering you felt. Do you see how you could be responsible for much of your own suffering by dwelling on it? This is "elected" suffering. The only place that painful event is taking place is in your mind. It is not presently real; it is a past experience.

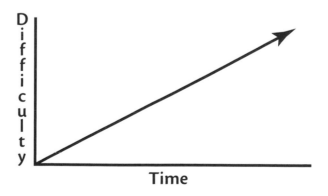

Now, imagine you are walking in a wooded forest when all of a sudden you hear a noise behind you. Instinctively you turn toward the sound. There, in the grass behind you, is a large snake that is about five feet long. You can tell it has been stalking you. Your turning around causes the snake to coil and begin to shake its rattle. You can't move. You're especially fascinated by the sight of the snake because of its color. You have never seen anything like it before. It is sky-blue with yellow stripes every four or five inches.

You step forward to look at this strange creature. Then it happens. Not the strike you were expecting, but something more frightening than that. You could not believe your eyes with the speed the snake moved. It simply disappeared....

Do you know why it disappeared? Because I stopped writing about it. I stopped creating a word picture in your mind. The snake was not real. But even more than that, let me call your attention to the fact that while you were focusing on the blue-and-yellow snake, you were not thinking about your painful childhood experience.

The human mind can only entertain one thought at a time. Granted, it can shift thoughts rapidly, but still only one thought can be focused on at a given moment. As you followed my promptings you changed your thought process. The same principle can be applied to your emotions if you desire to control them. You might respond, "That's just the power of positive thinking." To which I would respond, "You're correct. It is." Where do you think this power of positive thinking came from? It comes right out of the Bible.

On one occasion, the apostle Paul was incarcerated in a prison in Rome. He had been in prison before, and it was not much fun. While locked up he penned these words:

> Always be full of joy in the Lord; I say it again, rejoice!
> Let everyone see that you are unselfish and consid-

erate in all you do. Remember that the Lord is coming soon. Don't worry about anything; instead, pray about everything; tell God your needs, and don't forget to thank him for his answers. If you do this, you will experience God's peace, which is far more wonderful than the human mind can understand. His peace will keep your thoughts and your hearts quiet and at rest as you trust in Christ Jesus.

And now, brothers, as I close this letter, let me say this one more thing: Fix your thoughts on what is true and good and right. Think about things that are pure and lovely, and dwell on the fine, good things in others. Think about all you can praise God for and be glad about. Keep putting into practice all you learned from me and saw me doing, and the God of peace will be with you (Philippians 4:4-9).

Sure, we cannot change everything by thinking positive thoughts. I can't change the fact that my one daughter had a colostomy operation, my other daughter is a diabetic, my wife has had cancer removed from her body, or that I was in a head-on collision that almost took my life. These are "imposed" events that we had no control over. But we do have control over whether we become angry, resentful, or unforgiving. We must keep in mind the difference between *imposed* suffering and *elected* suffering.

There is nothing either good or bad, but thinking makes it so.

William Shakespeare

Register or Regulate? You Choose

In general, there are two types of people in this world: those who are controlled by life's events and circumstances, and those who attempt to control their lives and their destinies. The first could be likened to thermometers that *register* the temperature [atmosphere and events] around them. The others are like thermostats, which *regulate* the temperature [atmosphere and events] of their lives. The first group sees itself as a *victim* of circumstances, and the other sees itself as a *player* in the circumstances. Victims make excuses; players make changes. Victims think the events that occur in their lives are the important issue. Players believe that how they think about and respond to the events is more important than the events themselves. Victims think circumstances determine life and mental health. Players believe attitude determines life and mental health.

Victims	*Players*
Wishful thinking	Practical thinking
Immediate gratification	Delayed gratification
Ease	Work
Withdrawal	Involvement
Lack of goals	Goal setting
Powerless	Powerful
Give up easily	Persistent
Low self-esteem	Healthy self-esteem
Give in to temptation	Resist temptation
Discouraged	Enthusiastic
Undisciplined	Disciplined
Wait for opportunity	Create opportunity

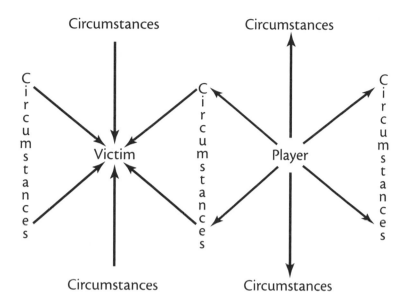

How Do You Feel Right Now?

In the first chapter we looked at the question, "What is going on?" This helped us focus on the various emotions and behaviors that tend to create bad or negative feelings. In this chapter, we have stimulated our thinking so we can determine how we are presently feeling. With this knowledge we can change our feelings by changing our thinking. But it is not enough to know what is bothering us and that we don't like it. How we respond is the key.

One response is to *deny* that problems exist. This is the "ostrich with the head in the sand" method. It doesn't resolve the conflict, it simply ignores the problem or the feelings. Another way is to *withdraw* from the problem or feeling. The person who is hurting simply walks—or runs—away from the situation. This "I don't want to talk about it" method buries the issue deeper into the recesses of the mind until it "festers." It is possible to acknowledge and deal with the problem through *compromise*. This is a sort of "get on with life" method. It usually only addresses some aspects of the problem, while leaving much of it unresolved. It also tends to frustrate those involved. The method that people fear most is *confrontation*. Confrontation faces the problem head-on and blasts through it. It carries with it the possibility of the death of a relationship or the separation and divorce of a marriage. It is this fear that causes people to choose the other mechanisms: to deny, to withdraw, or to compromise. How do you deal with the problems and feelings you experience? Has it been working for you? Do you want to continue it, or are you willing to stretch and grow a little by trying something new?

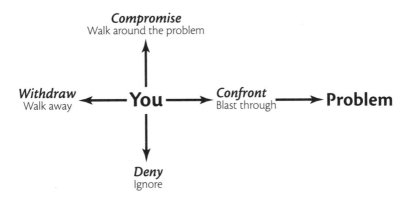

Don't run from pain because it is a good friend. It lets you know you are alive. It instructs you as to what is important. It tells you when something is not right. It is a great warning signal designed for your safety. Why is pain good? If you picked up a hot pan off the stove with your bare hands, you would feel pain. Is that pain initially a friend or an enemy? It is a friend if you listen and heed its warning. However, what was your friend can become your first-, second-, and third-degree enemy if you ignore it. What is true of physical pain is also true of emotional pain. At its first warning sign it is your friend alerting you to danger. If you deny, ignore, or try to compromise with this pain signal you will often get burned emotionally—sometimes very badly.

Life is filled with hurts and pain that we will not be able to change. We must then allow hurt and pain to change us.

Taking Action

Fill out the following evaluation to help you recognize problem areas.

Emotional Evaluation Quiz

1. I am feeling ❑ terrible ❑ bad ❑ sad ❑ frustrated ❑ satisfied ❑ happy ❑ terrific at this time in my life.

2. I am feeling hurt by a past event or situation in my life: ❑ yes ❑ no.

3. I am feeling hurt by a current event or situation in my life: ❑ yes ❑ no.

4. I am presently feeling hurt by a particular individual: ❑ yes ❑ no.

5. I have feelings of guilt over past or recent events or situations in my life: ☐ yes   ☐ no.

6. I am presently feeling angry with a particular person:
   ☐ yes   ☐ no.

7. I feel depressed   ☐ all the time   ☐ often
   ☐ occasionally   ☐ rarely.

8. I am presently feeling   ☐ satisfied   ☐ dissatisfied with my job.

9. I am presently feeling   ☐ satisfied   ☐ dissatisfied with the state of my mental health.

10. I am presently feeling   ☐ satisfied   ☐ dissatisfied with the state of my physical health.

11. I am presently feeling   ☐ satisfied   ☐ dissatisfied with the state of my spiritual health.

12. I have   ☐ healthy   ☐ unhealthy   relationships with my coworkers.

13. I have   ☐ happy   ☐ strained   relationships with my relatives.

14. I find myself worrying   ☐ often   ☐ occasionally
    ☐ rarely.

15. I experience anxiety thoughts   ☐ often   ☐ occasionally
    ☐ rarely.

16. I see myself as a person who responds   ☐ actively
    ☐ passively   to life's events.

17. There are people in my life that I resent and need to forgive: ☐ yes   ☐ no.

18. I have been entertaining thoughts that life is not worth living: ❐ yes ❐ no.

19. I would like to immediately change the following in my life:

20. Five years from now I would like to see the following changes take place in my life:

Do You Want to Change?

3

Change is what people fear most because all change represents loss of some kind; that's why we resist it so strongly.

GEORGE IS NOTHING BUT A couch potato. All he does is sit in front of the television set with the channel changer in his hand. I can't get him to do any yard work, and he won't do any type of exercise. I even have to do all the bookkeeping, pay the bills, and make the bank deposits. He is nothing but a lazy bum."

It was not hard to tell that Deena was unhappy with George. They had been in for several marital counseling sessions, but the sessions had gotten a little out of hand with both of them yelling. It was decided they would come in separately.

"Deena, last week when I was talking with George, he said that he would be willing to take over paying the bills so you would be relieved of that responsibility."

Before I could continue Deena said, "All he'll do is mess it up. He can't do anything right."

"I'm sure he will do a fine job. If he has any questions he can ask you."

"No way! He'll just get the checkbook and buy a new chair for himself to put in front of the TV."

It was evident that Deena did not want to alter her situation. Although her marriage was in trouble, the thought of giving up control of the checkbook was too great of a change. She would rather nurse her anger, resentment, and unforgiveness than transfer financial authority over to George.

WE USUALLY BELIEVE THAT WHEN people are unhappy or are living in difficult circumstances they will jump at the opportunity to change. But this is not the case; people resist change for many different reasons.

**The only one who likes change
is a newborn baby.**

The Five Fears

There are five major fears when it comes to the possibility of change. The first one is the *fear of the unknown*. There are no guarantees with change, so people have a tendency to resist anything new or unfamiliar. They worry about the possibility of more hurt, pain, or loss than they are presently experiencing.

Since they already are feeling a loss of direction and a sense of helplessness, they are not about to venture into any new, questionable areas. There is too much uncertainty involved. They prefer to quietly stay with the status quo—the known—even if it is a difficult situation. There is something familiar, even comfortable, about dealing with problems that we are accustomed to. No one wants to exchange one bad problem for another one.

There is also much insecurity with the unknown. When a person changes a job, experiences health issues, grows old, or retires, he or she is often fearful of moving into the areas of making new friends, dating, getting remarried, or encountering new situations. These fears can overwhelm people to the point of withdrawal.

Many live in dread of what is coming. Why should we? The unknown puts adventure into life....The unexpected around the corner gives a sense of anticipation and surprise. Thank God for the unknown future.

E. Stanley Jones

The second fear is the *fear of failure*. People do not want to fail, especially in front of others. That is why the number-one fear in the United States is that of public speaking. People want to be seen as in control, and, more than that, they like to have control of their own lives and the lives of other people. Also, no one wants to be seen as incompetent or a fool. No one wants to make the wrong decision or face the unpleasant task of telling other people that he or she was wrong. These involve severe loss of face. People will hang on to bad friendships rather than admit they made a mistake. They will endure terrible jobs rather than acknowledge they chose the wrong profession.

To admit we are wrong means acknowledging our errors in judgment and taking responsibility for them. That is a most difficult and unpleasant task. Eating crow is distasteful whether it is barbecued, baked, stewed, fried, or mashed.

**The person who succeeds is not
the one who holds back, fearing failure,
nor the one who never fails…but rather
the one who moves on in spite of failure.**

Chuck Swindoll

The third major fear of change is the *fear of rejection*. All human beings want to be liked. They desire to be accepted by family, friends, and business acquaintances. People seek approval from those around us. No one wants to be criticized or talked about. No one wants to be made fun of. Do you remember this little poem from your school days: "Sticks and stones may break my bones but names will never hurt me"? That is probably one of the biggest lies ever memorized by children. Of course mean names hurt us. People don't like to be gossiped about, slandered, or have their reputations destroyed. If we're honest, we would rather be struck with a rock than have our characters dismantled by words.

The reason most people do not confront others with the hurt they feel is because of the fear of rejection. Even battered women (or men) will stay in sick relationships out of a desire to be loved and accepted. The fear of rejection can paralyze people, keeping them from taking action or making needed changes.

**I find the pain of a little censure,
even when it is unfounded, is more
acute than the pleasure of much praise.**

Thomas Jefferson

These first three fears are the strongest; they are the most powerful reasons not to make changes. There are also two other fears that hamper change. One of them is the *fear of commitment*. This is often seen in the area of relationships with the opposite sex. To commit to another person is a risk and people tend to avoid risk taking. There are no guarantees that relationships will work out. There are no guarantees that we might not be deeply hurt if the relationships were severed for some reason. That would be very painful. This fear of hurt and loss stifle many people and keep them from stepping out by faith and making a commitment.

The fear of commitment can also be found in the area of employment. Some individuals are so concerned about finding the perfect job that they do not commit to any job...for fear that when the perfect job comes along, they will be locked into a job they hate.

People who cannot make commitments bounce from one job to another. Sometimes they bounce from one relationship to another. This fear of hurt and loss overpowers their lives and destroys their ability to make decisions. They oftentimes sabotage relationships and jobs to release themselves from the pressure and responsibility of commitment.

The last fear is the *fear of success*. As strange as it seems, some people are fearful of achieving. The concept of being successful is so foreign to them that the thought of flourishing overwhelms them. These individuals usually have low self-image; they cannot see themselves as successes. Being a failure, or maybe just average, is a familiar and comfortable way of life. Being a success would mean that their lifestyles would have to change. Being successful means they would have to face the fear of the unknown, the fear of rejection, and the burden and commitment to continue to succeed. Often this causes so much turmoil that they will disrupt their success. This gives them the freedom to return to the familiar territory of being average or even being failures.

**God may allow His servant to succeed when
He has disciplined him to a point where he
does not need to succeed to be happy.
The man who is elated by success and is
cast down by failure is still a carnal man.
At best his fruit will have a worm in it.**

A.W. Tozer

Life Is a River

Several years ago, I had the opportunity to raft down the Colorado River. The Colorado is a very large and swift body of water. During the 250-mile journey, we experienced over 200 white-water areas. These rapids are quite dangerous and exhilarating at the same time. But the reality is that much of the trip down the Colorado River is spent drifting on water that is swift but fairly calm.

Life is like one big, white-water adventure. Sometimes it is spent just drifting in the "dailyness" of living. Sometimes it is fast paced and overwhelming. We don't have the privilege of stopping the boat and getting off during the trip. We must face the big and small rapids and the still water whether we like it or not. There is no choice once we're on the river. We can either choose to be afraid of every ripple or learn to enjoy the refreshing splashes and the excitement of the deep drops into turbulent water.

What is your choice on the river? Have you been gritting your teeth and fighting the rapids? Have you come to a place where you want to stop fighting and start enjoying—to change?

Change is not an easy matter. It is often difficult and uncertain because life changes do not come with guarantees. However, change gives us the opportunity to grow. It enhances our experience of independence. Change can bring hope and the possibility of gaining control of an out-of-control situation. By facing change squarely in the face we can increase our self-esteem and diminish our fears.

The chart on the next page illustrates the concepts we have been looking at. In the center of the box there's a line that represents time. One arrow points to the past and the other arrow points to the future. The line that crosses the time line represents a passing of inner thoughts on one end and an outer expression of action on the other. It is one thing to think thoughts; it is another thing to express outward actions that everyone can see.

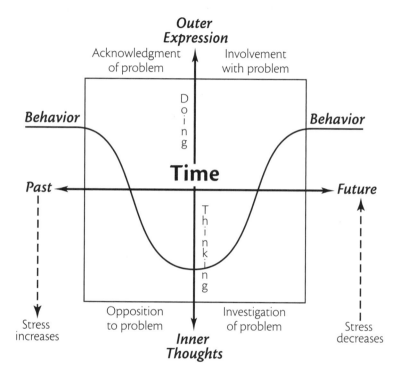

You will also notice four boxed in areas: Acknowledgment of problem, Opposition to problem, Investigation of problem, and Involvement with problem.

In chapters one and two, you *acknowledged* problems that may be current in your life. These are real issues that you are struggling with. Next, we looked at the *opposition* to your problem. This includes the various defense mechanisms and fears that arise in our thinking process. These fears may lead to denial or resistance in dealing with the issues causing our unhappiness. As we resist dealing with what is bothering us, our stress level increases. We begin to feel worse. If we keep focusing on the past we become stuck, and there is no forward movement or growth.

At some point in time, we need to become open to dealing with our problems and begin to *investigate* methods of resolving conflict. This intellectual exploration helps lead us to the next step. The final step is *involvement* with the problem, an actual working at resolving the issue. This is the outworking of taking what was a thinking process and putting on the "flesh and bones" of action. This is an actual change in behavior. As behavior begins to change, your stress level will decrease.

I am reminded of a story that James MacDonald shares in his book, *I Really Want to Change…So, Help Me, God*. It is the story of Raynald, who was a fourteenth century duke in Belgium. Raynald eventually became the king of Belgium, but his brother Edward was very jealous. Edward convinced a group to follow him and they overthrew Raynald's kingship. But Edward had compassion for Raynald and did not put him to death. Instead, he designed a special dungeon for him. It was a large circular room with one regular-sized doorway. It was outfitted with a bed, a table, and a chair. He included all the essentials that Raynald would need to be fairly comfortable.

When the dungeon was completely built *around* Raynald, Edward paid him a visit. Edward pointed to the regular-sized doorway and called Raynald's attention to the fact that there was no door in the opening. A door was not necessary to keep Raynald in the dungeon because he was grossly overweight and too fat to squeeze through the opening. Edward then said to Raynald, "When you can fit through the doorway, you can leave."

King Edward then instructed his servants to bring massive platters of meat and other delicacies and daily place them on the table in Raynald's round dungeon room. The servants also filled the table with various kinds of pies and pastries. Many people accused Edward of being cruel, but he would respond, "My brother is not a prisoner. He can leave when he chooses to."

Now for the rest of the story: "Raynald remained in that same room, a prisoner of his own appetite, for more than ten years. He wasn't released until after Edward died in battle. By then his own health was so far gone that he died within a year—not because he had no choice but because he would not use his power to choose what was best for his life."

This graphic story illustrates that even though people know what is wrong in their lives, it does not mean they will change. Sheer knowledge is not enough. It also illustrates that people can feel very badly about their circumstances and still not change. Feeling badly is not enough. People must choose to change. James 2:12-20, although talking primarily about good works, emphasizes the importance of taking action:

> You will be judged on whether or not you are doing what Christ wants you to. So watch what you do and what you think; for there will be no mercy to those who have shown no mercy. But if you have been merciful, then God's mercy toward you will win out over his judgment against you.
>
> Dear brothers, what's the use of saying that you have faith and are Christians if you aren't proving it by

helping others? Will that kind of faith save anyone? If you have a friend who is in need of food and clothing, and you say to him, "Well, good-bye and God bless you; stay warm and eat hearty," and then don't give him clothes or food, what good does that do?

So you see, it isn't enough just to have faith. You must also do good to prove that you have it. Faith that doesn't show itself by good works is no faith at all—it is dead and useless.

But someone may well argue, "You say the way to God is by faith alone, plus nothing; well, I say that good works are important too, for without good works you can't prove whether you have faith or not; but anyone can see that I have faith by the way I act."

Are there still some among you who hold that "only believing" is enough? Believing in one God? Well, remember that the demons believe this too—so strongly that they tremble in terror! Fool! When will you ever learn that "believing" is useless without doing what God wants you to? Faith that does not result in good deeds is not real faith.

Are you locked in a dungeon of emotional hurt and pain? Would you like to experience freedom? Then do something! Walk through the doorway! There is no door. There is no lock. The choice is yours. *Now, that's an awesome thought, isn't it?*

Personal Issues Chart

Place a check beside the issues you struggle with.

12 Major Addictive Struggles

❏ Alcoholism	❏ Lying
❏ Cheating	❏ Risk taking
❏ Drugs	❏ Shopping
❏ Eating problems	❏ Smoking
❏ Fighting	❏ Stealing
❏ Gambling	❏ Sexual lust

30 Common Personal Struggles

❏ Anger	❏ Laziness
❏ Anxiety	❏ Loneliness
❏ Bitterness	❏ Low self-image
❏ Boredom	❏ Negativity
❏ Criticalness	❏ Perfectionism
❏ Depression	❏ Pride
❏ Envy	❏ Procrastination
❏ Greed	❏ Profanity
❏ Grief	❏ Regret
❏ Gossip	❏ Resentment
❏ Guilt	❏ Sadness
❏ Hatred	❏ Self-pity
❏ Impatience	❏ Shyness
❏ Impulsiveness	❏ Unforgiveness
❏ Jealousy	❏ Worry

1. I struggle greatly with any changes that deal with the fear of the unknown: ☐ yes ☐ no ☐ occasionally.

2. I struggle greatly with any changes that deal with the fear of failure: ☐ yes ☐ no ☐ occasionally.

3. I struggle greatly with any changes that deal with the fear of rejection: ☐ yes ☐ no ☐ occasionally.

4. I struggle greatly with any changes that deal with the fear of commitment: ☐ yes ☐ no ☐ occasionally.

5. I struggle greatly with any changes that deal with the fear of success: ☐ yes ☐ no ☐ occasionally.

6. I have identified areas of personal struggle: ☐ yes ☐ no ☐ uncertain.

7. I have definitely become aware of feeling hurt, loss, and/or pain over my areas of struggle: ☐ yes ☐ no ☐ uncertain.

8. I want to make changes in my life: ☐ yes ☐ no ☐ uncertain.

People Only
Change When
They Hurt Enough

4

*All changes, even the most longed for, have their melancholy;
for what we leave behind us is a part of ourselves;
we must die to one life before we can enter into another.*

Anatole France

WHEN TOM ENTERED THE ROOM I could see he was under a great deal of stress. He walked slowly with a bent forward sort of lean and a downcast gaze. He melted into the chair and let out a deep sigh. His face was wrinkled and weather-beaten. He had the look of a much older man than his 43 years.

"Well, I've hit the bottom," he sighed. "This last month my boss fired me after I worked for him for 11 years. He said that he couldn't afford to have a drunk driving his warehouse trucks."

Tom had recently been in a major accident while driving under the influence of alcohol. Often he had driven company vehicles while drinking, but this time he was out of control and cost his employer a large sum of money. This loss of his job was the "straw that broke the camel's back." Two years earlier, his wife, Lacy, packed up their three children, moved back to her hometown, and divorced Tom because of his drinking.

Tom's drinking began in high school, got worse in college, and brought disaster when he was a young adult. He knew he had a problem, and he hated himself for the devastation he had brought to his family. He had tried many times to quit, but just couldn't follow through. He had finally come to the place where he had lost everything that mattered to him.

IT HAS BEEN ESTIMATED THAT less than 20 percent of people who are in financial, relational, or emotional trouble are willing to take any action to change their situations. Why? Because they have not come to the end of themselves. They haven't had enough pain. *People only change when they hurt enough.*

Why does negative behavior continue? It works. There is some kind of payoff, some type of momentary satisfaction that is derived from not changing. The reward might be financial or psychological. Some people will continue unproductive behavior to seek approval, acceptance, praise, or love. Others continue their unacceptable actions out of pride, greed, or a sense of personal fulfillment. They may oppress others with their need to always be right because they treasure being right—even if it destroys a relationship. The glutton king Raynald from Belgium is a classic example of this. His personal freedom did not mean as much to him as the instant gratification of something sweet in his mouth. His bizarre behavior continued because he did not suffer enough to become motivated to reduce. His freedom was only a few feet from the table of instant gratification.

We would rather be ruined than changed:
We would rather die in our dread
Than climb the cross of the moment
And let our illusions die.
W.H. Auden

Years ago I was a lifeguard. My job was to watch for swimmers who were in trouble and rescue them if necessary. It is easy to see the difference between a good swimmer and a bad swimmer. A good swimmer places one hand after another in the water following the center line of his or her body. The hand strokes seem to fall one on top of the other as they move forward.

A poor swimmer does not stroke following the center line. The person's hands hit the water right in front of each shoulder. When they get into trouble, their hand strokes begin to flail about, even going out to their sides. They are "grasping for straws" or anything that will keep them afloat.

A good lifeguard will not attempt to rescue a poor swimmer until he or she comes to the end of his or her strength and gives up. Rescuers know if they get too close, the swimmer will have enough strength to drown them in the midst of the rescue operation. The same is often true for those encountering emotional drowning. They must come to the place where they "hurt" enough to be helped. Jesus illustrated this principle when He told the story of the prodigal son.

> A man had two sons. When the younger told his father, "I want my share of your estate now, instead of

waiting until you die!" his father agreed to divide his wealth between his sons.

A few days later this younger son packed all his belongings and took a trip to a distant land, and there wasted all his money on parties and prostitutes. About the time his money was gone a great famine swept over the land, and he began to starve. He persuaded a local farmer to hire him to feed his pigs. The boy became so hungry that even the pods he was feeding the swine looked good to him. And no one gave him anything.

When he *finally came to his senses*, he said to himself, "At home even the hired men have food enough and to spare, and here I am, dying of hunger! I will go home to my father and say, 'Father, I have sinned against both heaven and you, and am no longer worthy of being called your son. Please take me on as a hired man.'"

So he returned home to his father. And while he was still a long distance away, his father saw him coming, and was filled with loving pity and ran and embraced him and kissed him.

His son said to him, "Father, I have sinned against heaven and you, and am not worthy of being called your son—"

But his father said to the slaves, "Quick! Bring the finest robe in the house and put it on him. And a jeweled ring for his finger; and shoes! And kill the calf we have in the fattening pen. We must celebrate with a feast, for this son of mine was dead and has returned to life. He was lost and is found." So the party began (Luke 15:11-24, emphasis added).

The prodigal son had to come to the *end* of his resources. He had to go to the pigpen before he was able to find relief for his situation. If he had been brought home before he had spent all of his money, he would have left home again. The prodigal's bankruptcy and hunger finally cleared up the fuzzy thinking caused by focusing all his energies on himself.

I count him braver who overcomes his desires than him who overcomes his enemies, for the hardest victory is victory over self.

Aristotle

Stepping Out

In reality, change is not an option. It is an ongoing, lifelong, daily experience. *How* we change is our only option. Change begins by choosing, and choosing creates more change. You, and you alone, are the author of the choice. What choices are you going to make? Why not ask God for wisdom to know exactly what changes He would like to make in you?

To make positive changes in your life you must begin by doing something differently—especially if what you are doing presently is not bringing happiness. You cannot ride a bike until you get on it. You can't learn to swim by standing on the shore. You can't catch a fish until you put the hook into the water. You can't eat carrots until you plant them. Talking about something does not bring results. There must be action. It is the cause-and-effect principle. "If you do different, you will have different. If you do the same, you will have the same." This is the sowing and reaping principle Paul talked about in Galatians 6:7-9.

> Don't be misled; remember that you can't ignore God and get away with it: a man will always reap just the kind of crop he sows! If he sows to please his own wrong desires, he will be planting seeds of evil and he will surely reap a harvest of spiritual decay and death; but if he plants the good things of the Spirit, he will reap the everlasting life that the Holy Spirit gives him. And let us not get tired of doing what is right, for after a while we will reap a harvest of blessing if we don't get discouraged and give up.

It is by action that men and women define themselves. She is a mother because she mothers. He is a carpenter because he builds houses. She is a soccer player because she plays. No one is a mother, carpenter, or soccer player without the accompanying actions. We are what we do.

**The actions of men are the
best interpreters of their thoughts.**
John Locke

I am an angry person because I hold and display angry thoughts and actions. I am a depressed person because I display hopeless thoughts and actions. I am a critical person because I display critical thoughts and actions. We cannot separate the two. Jesus even said, "All of you listen...and try and understand. Your souls aren't harmed by what you eat, but by what you think and say!...It is the thought-life that pollutes. For from within, out of men's hearts, come evil thoughts of lust, theft, murder, adultery, wanting what belongs to others, wickedness, deceit, lewdness, envy, slander, pride, and all other folly. All these vile things come from within; they are what pollute you and make you unfit for God" (Mark 7:14,15,20-23).

It is our minds that think either positive thoughts or negative thoughts. We can think about how much we resent people or how much we appreciate them. We can dwell on the unfairness of our circumstances or the blessings in our circumstances. We can see a thorn with every rose or a rose with every thorn. We can see a difficulty with every opportunity or an opportunity with every difficulty.

The mind is like the engine on a train. It gives direction to our thinking and behavior. The will is the motivator for the engine. It is the coal car supplying energy to the mind. The will is extremely powerful; it can override the promptings of the mind and force action in a different path than was originally chosen. For example, I have had the wonderful opportunity to travel to many different places. Often I have been served food that was foreign to my experience. My mind has argued, *Don't eat that. There's no telling what will happen or how bad it will taste.* However, my will has overridden my mind, and I have eaten armadillo in Bolivia, ostrich in Uganda, and sheep fat in Mongolia.

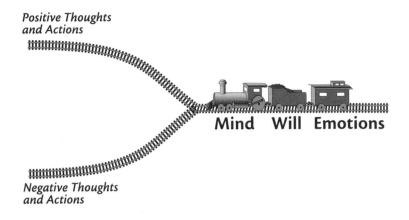

Positive Thoughts and Actions

Mind   Will   Emotions

Negative Thoughts and Actions

The feelings are like the caboose on the train. They follow where the mind and will lead. If they lead emotions down happy tracks, the feelings will be happy. If they lead emotions down unhappy tracks, the feelings will be unhappy. Often the feelings shout out which direction to go, but if we let our feelings choose our track we may find ourselves on an unpleasant detour.

As science has proven, an object that is in motion tends to stay in motion. This is also true for our emotions. Negative emotions tend to stimulate and keep in motion negative emotions; positive emotions stimulate and keep in motion more positive emotions. We can see this in the physical realm, also. If we start a jogging program and keep it up for a period of time, it creates the desire to continue jogging. Our bodies will begin to miss jogging on those occasions when we are unable to complete a workout.

Thinking Is Not Action

Thinking about doing something is not the same as doing it. Thinking about stealing is not stealing. Thinking about dishonesty is not the same as lying. One can lead to the other, but they are not the same. You can say that both are wrong (and they are), but thinking about breaking something is not the same as doing it.

Often people think about doing the right thing. They dwell on those thoughts and evaluate just the best way to do the right thing—but they never take action! I call this "Aristotelian" logic. Aristotle used *deductive* logic to come to his conclusions. This is the process of creating propositions in terms of their forms [abstract or general] instead of their content [actual and specific].

Our society is filled with Aristotelian logic. For example, would you like to be able to play the piano? I mean just sit down and play almost any tune that comes to your mind. Wouldn't it be fun to be the life of the party and lead others in group singing or maybe even play in a concert? Possibly you would prefer to just quietly play for yourself for sheer enjoyment. You might even entertain the thought of creating your own songs for others to enjoy. Wouldn't that be a wonderful talent to have?

I am sure there would be a host of people who would raise their hands and say, "I'd like to be able to play the piano. It would be fun. I would really like to do it." That is an example of Aristotelian logic. It has become a little warped from Aristotle's original intention, but it is part of the fabric of American society. In a nutshell it says, "Since I *think* I would like to play the piano, and since I *feel* like I would like to play the piano, it is true. It is reality. Conclusion: I would like to play the piano."

Deductive reasoning is the belief that if I repeat something often enough, it will become true in my mind. That is why some people who exaggerate and lie long enough begin to believe their own falsehoods as truth.

There is another form of thinking that I call "Hebraic" logic. Rather than using deduction and starting at the beginning and coming to a conclusion, this method uses the concept of *induction*. It looks at a specific or particular thought or activity and then begins to make a general conclusion.

Let's go back to the piano. The individual who would be using Hebraic logic would ask, "Do you play the piano?" [specific and pointed]. "No, but I would like to" [general and abstract]. At which point the one using Hebraic logic would say, "No, you really would not like to play. For if you really wanted to play the piano…you would. You would put forth the effort to practice. As a result of your practice, you would play the piano." Conclusion: You don't really want to play or you would.

Hebraic logic basically says, "Actions speak louder than words. What you are speaks so loudly that I can't hear what you are saying. Don't talk the walk if you don't walk the talk."

**Thought is the blossom; language the bud;
action the fruit behind it.**

Ralph Waldo Emerson

Life Rewards Action

Life does not compensate us for insight, understanding, wisdom, or intention. It only rewards action. I can tell the Internal Revenue Service that I intended to pay my taxes, but all they care about is the money. I can tell my wife that I understand how tired she is, but she would appreciate more my doing the dishes. I can tell my mechanic that I have gained much insight as to how an internal combustion engine runs, but all he will ask is, "Did you put oil in it?" I can tell my children that I read a book and acquired much wisdom on being a father, but all they care about is if I attend their soccer game. Henry Ford said, "You can't build a reputation on what you intend to do." It is so easy to get wrapped up in mind games and forget practical, daily living.

There has always been a battle between what we should be doing in life and what we actually end up doing. Paul addresses this in Romans 7:15-23.

> I don't understand myself at all, for I really want to do what is right, but I can't. I do what I don't want to— what I hate. I know perfectly well that what I am doing is wrong, and my bad conscience proves that I agree with these laws I am breaking. But I can't help myself because I'm no longer doing it. It is sin inside me that is stronger than I am that makes me do these evil things.

> I know I am rotten through and through so far as my old sinful nature is concerned. No matter which way I turn I can't make myself do right. I want to but I can't. When I want to do good, I don't; and when I try not to do wrong, I do it anyway. Now if I am doing what I don't want to, it is plain where the trouble is: sin still has me in its evil grasp.

> It seems to be a fact of life that when I want to do what is right, I inevitably do what is wrong. I love to do God's will so far as my new nature is concerned; but there is something else deep within me, in my lower nature, that is at war with my mind and wins the fight and makes me a slave to the sin that is still

within me. In my mind I want to be God's willing servant, but instead I find myself still enslaved to sin. So you see how it is: my new life tells me to do right, but the old nature that is still inside me loves to sin. Oh, what a terrible predicament I'm in! Who will free me from my slavery to this deadly lower nature? Thank God! It has been done by Jesus Christ our Lord. He has set me free.

How do we begin to deal with our problems? Some schools of thought would say, "We need to find the root of the problem. We need to dredge through the garbage dump of our past and find the original causes to what's bothering us now."

I realize that some insight and important information can be gained by looking through the past. However, the more important issue is what is presently going on in your life and what you want to change for the future.

Let's say that you and I were in the mountains admiring the beautiful rocks and trees. All of a sudden we heard a noise and looked up. It was the sound of an avalanche. Huge boulders were rolling down the mountain toward us. We are standing in the pathway and will most likely soon be crushed to death.

With a frightened look you turn to me. I respond by saying, "Be calm. All we have to do is to find out what started the avalanche, and we will be safe. We need to find the root cause for why those rocks started rolling toward us."

You respond by saying, "You're out of your mind! What we need to do is start running for our lives from the biggest boulders!"

You would be absolutely correct. It is only after we are safe from the biggest boulders that we can take the time to determine how it all got started. And maybe then, when we were safe from the biggest boulders, it wouldn't even matter how they all got started. Probably a more important issue would be how to escape from boulders and how to not get any more rolling.

What are the big boulders in your life? Are you scared enough to run for your life? Have you been "hurt" enough to change?

I REMEMBER TALKING TO ONE individual about a pressing situation in his life. I listened to his story for a while and then said, "I don't think you've hurt enough yet." I could see the look of shock on his face. *Of course I'm hurting*, he thought. I went on to say, "When you hurt enough you will change."

Let's say you and I were standing in a parking lot talking. During the course of our conversation I hit you on your shoulder. The punch caught you off guard. *What is he doing*, you think to yourself. Our talk continues, and I hit you again. You think, *How dare he hit me. Who does he think he is?* It isn't long before I hit you again. This time you back away from me. We keep on talking, and I hit you a fourth time.

How many hits would you take before you would say to me, "Knock it off!" The truth of the matter is, you would tell me to stop when you got sick and tired of me hitting you. Are you sick and tired of taking emotional hits? When you are, you will change. If you're not quite to that place yet, it's okay. You're in process. You just need to hurt a little more because *people only change when they hurt enough*.

I'm reminded of the story of the young man who wanted to become very wise. He traveled all over the world talking with people. One day he heard there was an extremely wise man who lived in the mountains of Mexico.

After many days of travel, the young man came upon the house of the wise man. He knocked and the old man opened the door. The young man introduced himself and asked the old man if he was the wise man he was looking for. The old man carefully looked at the young man and said, "Perhaps."

For several days the young man told his story of his search for wisdom. The old man listened quietly. Finally the young man ran out of words and said, "Do you have any wise thoughts for me?"

The old man said, "Perhaps." He then motioned for the young man to follow him. They walked down a path toward a beautiful lake.

Upon arriving the young man said, "This is breathtaking. Is this where I can obtain wisdom?"

"Perhaps," said the old man.

The old man took the young man to the side of the lake and said, "Bend over and look carefully into the dark water." The young man got on his knees, bent over, and peered into the water. He could see his own face in the reflection of the still water. Suddenly, the old man pushed the young man's head under water. He struggled to break free but could not because the old man was very strong. Soon he could feel himself starting to lose consciousness from the lack of air.

At that point, the old man pulled the young man's head out of the water. The young man gasped for air and yelled, "What are doing! You almost killed me! You're crazy!"

"Perhaps," said the old man. "But when you truly search for wisdom as you were fighting for air, then you will become wise."

My dear reader, when you seek emotional health and freedom from your hurt and pain as you would fight for air—then you too will change.

My Favorite Excuses

What is your favorite excuse for putting off change in your life?
What phrases do you use to convince yourself not to get started?
What self-talk comments best describe your habit for avoiding dif-
ficult tasks or situations? Place a check by the comments that best
describe your excuse pattern. (You may even find several that
qualify as your favorites.)

❏ I'm too busy.

❏ I'm too old.

❏ I'm too tired.

❏ I'm too young.

❏ I'm doing okay.

❏ I'm not sure I have the energy.

❏ I'm really not good at that.

❏ I'm just not up to it.

❏ I'm not feeling good.

❏ I'm not smart enough.

❏ I'm comfortable where I'm at.

❏ I'm overwhelmed.

❏ I'm not that organized.

❏ I'm a procrastinator.

❏ I'm not cut out for that.

❏ I'm quiet by nature.

❏ I'm just too lazy.

❏ I'm waiting for the right moment.

❒ I'm waiting for them to say they are sorry.

❒ I don't have the time right now.

❒ I don't want to.

❒ I can't afford it

❒ I don't have the willpower.

❒ I don't have the strength.

❒ I don't think I could do it.

❒ I don't think it will work.

❒ I don't need any more pain.

❒ I don't need any more stress.

❒ I have better things to do.

❒ I don't deserve this.

❒ I never have any luck.

❒ I have more important things to deal with.

❒ I don't think I could pull it off.

❒ I don't want to work that hard.

❒ I don't have any choice.

❒ I like it the way it is.

❒ I have enough worries.

❒ I don't want to talk about it.

❒ I just can't do it.

❒ I can't break the habit.

❒ I don't have any concentration.

❒ I can't help it.

- ❏ I don't deserve happiness.
- ❏ I don't want to be a hypocrite.
- ❏ I can't deal with this right now.
- ❏ I can never do anything right.
- ❏ I think I'm going crazy.
- ❏ I can't handle any more.
- ❏ I don't want an argument.
- ❏ I've got too many responsibilities.
- ❏ I've been hurt enough already.
- ❏ I've never been good at anything.
- ❏ I've tried it before, and it doesn't work.
- ❏ I've been there before.
- ❏ I've had it.
- ❏ I've been a loser all my life.
- ❏ I'll just quit again.
- ❏ I'll just get mad.
- ❏ It will never work.
- ❏ It won't do any good.
- ❏ It's too big of a task.
- ❏ It's just a dead end.
- ❏ It's just going through the motions.
- ❏ It's just my upbringing.
- ❏ It's just my personality.
- ❏ It's just not fair.

- ☐ It's not my fault.
- ☐ It's just been one of those days.
- ☐ It's not my problem.
- ☐ You just don't understand.
- ☐ You can't teach an old dog new tricks.
- ☐ You have no idea what I've been going through.
- ☐ Not today.
- ☐ Maybe tomorrow.
- ☐ That's not for me.
- ☐ Maybe when I'm feeling better.
- ☐ That's just the way I am.
- ☐ Leave me alone.
- ☐ Someday.
- ☐ Once the kids get out of the home…
- ☐ Later.
- ☐ Convince me.
- ☐ My brain can't handle it now.
- ☐ No way.
- ☐ No one listens to me anyway.
- ☐ Nothing ever changes.
- ☐ Why don't you change the subject?
- ☐ Only the rich succeed.
- ☐ No matter what I do, it won't make any difference.

When I look at the excuses I've checked, the following general pattern best describes my behavior in dealing with problems:

As I look at my excuse system—

1. I am satisfied with the way I am: ❐ yes   ❐ no.

2. I don't think I have the power to change:
   ❐ true   ❐ false.

3. I have not come to the point of hurting enough to change: ❐ true   ❐ false.

4. I sincerely desire to change: ❐ yes   ❐ no.

5. I will make a definite commitment to change:
   ❐ yes   ❐ no.

6. I will start the change process today: ❐ yes   ❐ no.

Dear God,

I am the king (queen) of excuses. I've tried all of them, but none of them have brought happiness. I'm tired of all the pain, hurt, and suffering I've been feeling. I know I can't make the changes by myself. I've tried time and again, and it only ends in failure. I desperately need Your help. I need Your strength. I need Your encouragement. Please hear my cry and come to my aid. I've come to the end of my resources like the prodigal son did. I'm tired of the pigpen. I'm looking forward to coming home to Your open arms. Amen.

Making Peace with Pain Is the Way to Healing

Have courage for the great sorrows of life and patience for the small ones; and when you have laboriously accomplished your daily task, go to sleep in peace. God is awake.

Victor Hugo

IT STARTED OUT AS A NORMAL DAY. The sun was shining, and I was busy as usual. I was just about to step on the platform to speak to a youth group in Southern California when I heard, "Bob, you've got a phone call."

It was my wife, Pam. I could tell she was distraught and trying to hold herself together. She proceeded to tell me that our youngest daughter, Christy, was in the hospital in Fresno. I was floored when she told me that Christy was in a diabetic coma. I couldn't believe it; she was not quite four years of age.

It was a long and difficult drive home. During the four-and-a-half-hour trip, I was overcome with helplessness. Tears streamed down my face as I struggled with keeping the speed limit even though my daughter was near death.

Pain runs deep in a parent's heart who stands beside the bed of their child in deep danger. How we long to take away his or her hurt, but we cannot. A mother and father can only draw close together, cry, and pray. When disability comes to one family member, it affects all of them. Everyone must work through their own emotions and adjust to reality. In the case of juvenile diabetes, the physical reality is constantly testing blood sugar. The blood is drawn four to six times a day, and insulin shots must be given when necessary.

In the midst of all of this adjustment, tragedy struck again. Six months after the coma Christy was playing with some friends as I drove up in our car. I rolled down my window and spoke to the children. Then they saw a horse riding by, and they ran to take a look. I drove on.

Little did I know that Christy had turned back and ran to the car. It was a four door sedan, and she grabbed hold of one of the back-door handles. She was holding on and running beside the car. I was watching the road ahead and another car coming toward me. Then it happened. She tripped and got pulled under the car. You can only barely imagine how I felt running over my own daughter. I get sick just writing down these words. We came close to losing her twice within six months.

Over the years, our family has experienced much emotional, financial, and physical pain. It hurts to trust friends only to find they mismanaged our money invested in a land development program. We had borrowed on our home and lost it all because of their greed and dishonesty. Because I don't believe in bankruptcy, it took us 17 years to pay back the borrowed money.

Several years ago a man in a pickup ran a stop sign. His actions forced me into a head-on accident that nearly took my life. I was taken to the hospital by helicopter because my body systems were shutting down. I recovered after a period of time only to face the reality of constant pain in both of my hands and wrists.

I am not going to list every one of my painful or hurtful experiences. I have only shared these to let you know I have not lived a life of ease. My family, like many others, has had its portion of problems. I am sure that you, too, could share personal stories of suffering and pain.

We don't have to look far to see vast amounts of heartache and despair. Newspapers and television programs are filled with stories of fire, flood, earthquakes, and tornados. Natural disasters have disrupted many families worldwide. Theft, murder, rape, child abuse, and other crimes have ripped up the lives of millions. Drugs and alcohol continue to destroy individuals and their loved ones. Cancer, heart disease, and other illnesses strike new people every day. It has become common to hear of people being laid off of work, friends facing the devastation of an accident, or loved ones going through divorce. The pain of broken or damaged relationships has been experienced by every one of us.

I know of no one who is not hurting in some form or fashion. You might respond by saying, "Bob, I'm not hurting." To which I would simply say, "Cheer up—you soon will be." Pain and suffering are part of the life experience. We would prefer a beautiful rose garden, but that is not the way it is. Life is difficult. We cannot avoid the shock of accident or injury. We cannot escape the discomfort of sickness or loss. We cannot dodge the anguish of broken relationships. We cannot run away from the sadness of the death of a loved one. We cannot evade the stabbing irritation of hurtful comments.

Since there is no escape from the various forms of suffering that humanity experience, what are we to do? We must learn to face the pain. Evading or running away will not solve anything. We need to confront and work on legitimate suffering.

**Once we truly know that life is difficult—
once we truly understand and accept it—
then life is no longer difficult.
Because once it is accepted, the fact that
life is difficult no longer matters.**

M. Scott Peck

To better understand this concept, it is important to note the difference between imposed suffering versus elected suffering. Imposed suffering is comprised of life events over which we have no control. Natural disasters would be a classic example. We have no control over earthquakes and the damage they produce. We have no control over who will become a Type I diabetic. We have no control over those who would fire us or lay us off of work. All of these experiences are imposed or forced upon us from the outside. We cannot change them. We can only painfully accept them and move on.

Elected suffering still creates agony, but it comes from a different source. It is not imposed because it comes from inside us. It is created out of our own thinking process or our own actions. No one forces us to become alcoholics; we choose to drink. No one forces drugs upon us; we choose to take drugs. No one forces us to overeat; we choose to put food in our mouths. No one forces us to divorce our spouses; we choose to divorce our spouses. We choose to look at pornography. We choose to lie. We choose to steal. We choose to cheat. We choose to gossip. We choose to be negative and critical. We choose to be bitter and angry. We choose to hurt others. The responsibility for the pain and misery that comes from elected suffering is ours and ours alone.

Serenity Prayer
God, grant me the serenity
to accept the things I cannot change,
the courage to change the things I can,
and the wisdom to know the difference.

Another way to look at our choices is that there are facts of life and there are problems of life. Facts are the things we cannot change. For example, I cannot change the fact that my wife had cancer. I cannot change the fact that my oldest daughter has had to undergo a colostomy due to the mistake of a doctor. I cannot change the fact that I have had to bury both of my parents. I cannot change the fact of constant pain. None of the above are problems for me; they are simply facts of life. To be angry or fight against them is fruitless.

Problems are different than facts. Problems can be worked on. They can be overcome or changed. Overeating is a problem. Anger is a problem. Fear is a problem. Worry is a problem. Depression is a problem. Having a critical spirit is a problem. Problems give us the opportunity to make changes in our thinking and behavior. When we take responsibility for our problems, we can change and grow. When responsibility is shouldered it creates hope. Hope generates energy and gives motivation to solve problems.

**Life is either a daring adventure or nothing.
Security does not exist in nature,
nor do the children of men as a whole
experience it. Avoiding danger is
no safer in the long run than exposure.**
Helen Keller

What is your outlook toward problems? Are you willing to face them? Are you willing to learn from them and grow in maturity? The Bible gives much encouragement for those who want to learn how to deal with problems and difficulties:

We can rejoice, too, when we run into problems and trials, for we know that they are good for us—they help us learn to be patient. And patience develops strength of character in us and helps us trust God more each time we use it until finally our hope and faith are strong and steady. Then, when that happens, we are able to hold our heads high no matter what happens and know that all is well, for we know how dearly God loves us, and we feel this warm love everywhere within us because God has given us the Holy Spirit to fill our hearts with his love (Romans 5:3-5).

What a wonderful God we have—he is the Father of our Lord Jesus Christ, the source of every mercy, and the one who so wonderfully comforts and strengthens us in our hardships and trials. And why does he do this? So that when others are troubled, needing our sympathy and encouragement, we can pass on to them this same help and comfort God has given us. You can be sure that the more we undergo suffering for Christ, the more he will shower us with his comfort and encouragement (2 Corinthians 1:3-5).

Dear brothers, is your life full of difficulties and temptations? Then be happy, for when the way is rough, your patience has a chance to grow. So let it grow, and don't try to squirm out of your problems. For when your patience is finally in full bloom, then you will be ready for anything, strong in character, full and complete (James 1:2-4).

So be truly glad! There is wonderful joy ahead, even though the going is rough for a while down here. These trials are only to test your faith, to see whether or not it is strong and pure. It is being tested as fire tests gold and purifies it—and your faith is far more precious to God than mere gold; so if your faith remains strong after being tried in the test tube of fiery trials, it will bring you much praise and glory and honor on the day of his return (1 Peter 1:6,7).

God Is Sovereign

The Refiner's Fire

He sat by the fire of sevenfold heat,
    As He watched by the precious ore,
And closer He bent with a searching gaze
    As He heated it more and more.
He knew He had ore that could stand the test,
    And He wanted the finest gold

To mould as a crown for the King to wear,
    Set with gems with price untold.
So He laid our gold in the burning fire,
    Tho' we fain would have said to Him, "Nay,"
And He watched the dross that we had not seen,
    And it melted and passed away.
And the gold grew brighter and yet more bright,
    But our eyes were so dim with tears,
We saw but the fire—not the Master's hand,
    And questioned with anxious fears.
Yet our gold shone out with a richer glow,
    As it mirrored a Form above,
That bent o'er the fire, tho' unseen by us,
    With a look of ineffable love.
Can we think that it pleases His loving heart
    To cause us a moment's pain?
Ah, no! But He saw through the present cross
    The bliss of eternal gain.
So He waited there with a watchful eye,
    With a love that is strong and sure,
And His gold did not suffer a bit more heat,
    Than was needed to make it pure.

Author Unknown

This poem highlights one of the most important doctrines of the Bible—the sovereignty of God. God is all-knowing and all-powerful. He is in control of the affairs of man. God is not caught off guard by any of the problems or trials we face. He knows the beginning and ending of all of our stories. God is not frustrated, overwhelmed, or thwarted by evil or any of our thoughts and actions. God is supreme and has power over this world and the universe.

Understanding the sovereignty of God helps bring peace in the midst of the great storms of life. Knowing that God is sovereign deepens our awe and fear of Him. It provides a solid foundation that cannot be shaken regardless of the problems we face. God's sovereignty gives us the assurance that He is aware of our struggles and will comfort us. Believing in God's absolute control helps us create an attitude of acceptance and thankfulness. When we realize that God's timing is not wrong for us, we discover trust and security. We know that in God's great plan He will lead us through the valley of the shadow of death. We will fear no evil.

Have you made peace with pain? Have you come to the place where you have accepted the facts of life that cannot be changed? Or are you still fighting and holding on thinking they will change? Is it time for you to let go? Is it time for you to submit to the bridle and bit of reality?

Remember the difference between facts of life and problems? Problems can be worked on. Maybe there are some issues in your life that need a little work. Maybe it is your temper or lack of self-control. It might be in the area of procrastination or organization. It could be that you struggle with a low self-image or strong perfectionist tendencies. Whatever difficulty you are facing, today is the day to get started on effecting change.

**Moaning over your troubles is silly.
Few persons ever listen to you, and
those who do are not apt to like the sound.**

I'm reminded of the story of the man who was complaining about all of his problems. He moaned and groaned that the cross of trials he had to bear was too difficult.

"I would sure like to get rid of this cross," he said one day.

"Zap!" All of a sudden he was ushered into heaven and found himself standing before St. Peter. "What am I doing here?" he asked. "Did I die?"

"No," said St. Peter. "I just heard you complaining about your cross, and I thought I would help you out. Come with me to the Warehouse of Crosses. We'll see if we can find you a new one."

The man followed St. Peter to a large warehouse that was filled with crosses. There were big crosses and little crosses. Wooden crosses and glass crosses. There were even some heavy metal crosses. There were crosses of all colors, shapes, and forms. There was even a large cross on wheels.

St. Peter said, "You can go anywhere in the warehouse you like and select the cross of your choice."

"Wow! That's a great plan," said the man.

He began walking through the warehouse looking at all the crosses. It took him hours before he finally found one to his liking. It was a very small and light aluminum cross. He took it back to St. Peter for approval.

"A great choice," said St. Peter. "That's the very same cross you've been carrying."

Someone said, "There is no such thing as a problem that doesn't have a gift in it." Are you ready to discover that gift?

Experiencing a great sorrow is like entering a cave. We are overwhelmed by the darkness and the loneliness. We feel that there is no escape from the prison-house of pain. But God in His lovingkindness has placed on the invisible wall the lamp of faith, whose beams shall lead us back to the sunlit world, where work and friends and service await us.

Helen Keller

Taking Action

I am dealing with the following difficult issue:

This issue has the following facts that I need to accept even though I might not like them:

This issue has the following problems that I can work on:

The first thing I am planning to do is:

I plan to get started:

Date _____

Dear God,

I have been dealing with a lot of pain and hurt in my life. I have been fighting against difficult facts. I'm ready to submit and accept the things I cannot change. This has been a hard battle, and I need Your help to make it a reality.

Please help me get started on the problems I can work on and change. I realize this may be harder than making peace with the difficult facts. I can already feel the weight of personal responsibility, and I want to run from it. Please infuse me with courage to change negative habits and negative ways of thinking. Help me become a disciplined person. Amen.

Being Honest Is the Starting Place for Growth

6

Never give 'em more than one barrel to start with. But if they are foolish enough to ask for more, then give 'em the other barrel right between the eyes.

John Wesley Dafoe

W**E ESTIMATE THAT YOU'VE GOT** about three months to live," said Dr. MacArthur. "The tests indicate a very rapidly moving type of liver cancer."

How would you like to hear these words? Would it send shock waves into your system of thinking? Would you begin to seriously evaluate your life and priorities? Would it change how you interacted with your family, friends, and work associates? Would you rather be kept in the dark than face the pain and reality of your soon departure?

I am of the firm conviction that most people would rather hear the truth than be lied to. No matter how difficult or painful truth might be, it is better than deceit. I don't relish the thought of being told that I have bad breath or broccoli stuck in my teeth. But I prefer the truth to the realization that I spent the entire day staggering people with my breath or showing off chewed-up greenery. It is better to be told that we have something hanging out of our noses than to look into a mirror after an important business meeting and see the offending object ourselves.

It's time to take an honest look at your life. It might be painful and disconcerting, but in the end the truth will set you free. Are you generally happy with the life you have been living? Are you ready to make a change?

Recognizing Consequences

As we've discussed earlier, the facts of life are things we cannot change, such as natural disasters, accidents, or crippling illnesses. We must come to the point of resignation and acceptance with those. The changes I'm referring to deal with the problems of life that can be altered: damaged relationships, careers, where we live, where we go to school, personal finances. We can work on our attitudes, our weight, and our laziness. We can stop smoking, drinking, or taking drugs. We can quit lying, blaming, and rebelling. We can choke off pornography, adultery, and sexual addiction. We can silence our anger, worry, and fear. We can break away from our depression, low self-image, and loneliness. We can defeat negative thinking, perfectionism, and pride. We can bring family arguments to an end.

The life you are presently living is a result of your choices. If you are not happy now, it follows that you haven't been making good choices. If you want to move your life in a positive direction, you must change your decisions. How different would your life be if you had chosen not to become angry and say the hurtful things you said to a loved one? Where would you be today financially if you hadn't chosen to get involved with that multilevel marketing program? What difference would there be in your weight if you had chosen to work out rather than sit in front of the television eating Twinkies and Ding Dongs? Would you have done better on the test if you had chosen to study rather than to party with your friends?

Sometimes I will be counseling people and they will say, "I just can't choose. I can't change! That's just the way I am." My usual response is, "Can't or won't?" Avoiding personal responsibility is just another way to say, "I'm not going to change." We *can* change if we want to. All our choices have consequences, whether they are large or small. When you choose the thought, you choose the consequences. When you choose the action or behavior, you choose the consequences. In physics we were taught about cause and effect—for every action there is an equal and opposite reaction. In the Bible this is called the law of sowing and reaping. Galatians 6:7-9 says:

> Don't be misled; remember that you can't ignore God and get away with it: a man will always reap just the kind of crop he sows! If he sows to please his own wrong desires, he will be planting seeds of evil and he will surely reap a harvest of spiritual decay and death; but if he plants the good things of the Spirit, he will reap the everlasting life that the Holy Spirit gives him. And let us not get tired of doing what is right, for after a while we will reap a harvest of blessing if we don't get discouraged and give up.

We are accountable and responsible for the life we live. We can't sow slothfulness and expect a harvest of discipline. We can't sow bitterness and expect a harvest of happiness. We can't sow worry and expect a harvest of peace. We can't sow jealousy and expect a harvest of trust. We can't sow turmoil and expect a harvest of joy. What we sow, what we choose, determines how our lives will go.

Managing our lives begins with learning to manage ourselves and our choices. No one forces us to choose the wrong direction. We love to blame people, things, and situations outside of ourselves for the lack of fulfillment of our dreams, but the ugly truth is that we are the ones who made the choices.

The Process of Thoughts, Decisions, Actions, and Results

Temptation Circumstances Heredity Influences Environment Past Experiences	impact thoughts and the thinking process	that leads to decisions or choices	which produce actions and behavior	that result in positive or negative consequences

Often we make poor choices because we want immediate gratification. We want the choice of immediate satisfaction of eating pizza now rather than the delayed gratification of losing weight, which takes self-denial, time, and physical exercise. We choose to yell and throw tantrums because we want our way at once rather than the delayed gratification of working at a relationship.

Think about someone training for the Olympics. How often do they deny their immediate desires for the goal of winning? How much self-discipline do they exercise to become the best they can be? Think about how many hours, days, and months they exercise and practice for a few moments of glory. These athletes make choices that will affect their future in a positive way. Paul the Apostle touches on this subject when he says in 1 Corinthians 9:24-27:

> In a race everyone runs, but only one person gets first prize. So run your race to win. To win the contest you must deny yourselves many things that would keep you from doing your best. An athlete goes to all this trouble just to win a blue ribbon or a silver cup, but we do it for a heavenly reward that never disappears. So I run straight to the goal with purpose in every step. I fight to win. I'm not just shadow-boxing or playing around. Like an athlete I punish my body, treating it roughly, training it to do what it should, not what it wants to. Otherwise I fear that after enlisting others for the race, I myself might be declared unfit and ordered to stand aside.

Let's consider some possible reasons for not making good choices as a starting point. One reason you have been struggling with positive choices may be your relationship with God. It is possible that you have grown up knowing about Him *intellectually* but not *personally*. It is only when we receive Christ into our hearts that our lives are changed. God comes into our lives through His Holy Spirit and brings eternal life and the ability to cope with problems and overcome temptation. Paul the Apostle describes this transaction in Romans 10:8-13.

> For salvation that comes from trusting Christ—which is what we preach—is already within easy reach of each of us; in fact, it is as near as our own hearts and mouths. For if you tell others with your own mouth that Jesus Christ is your Lord and believe in your own heart that God has raised him from the dead, you will be saved. For it is by believing in his heart that a man becomes right with God; and with his mouth he tells

others of his faith, confirming his salvation. For the Scriptures tell us that no one who believes in Christ will ever be disappointed. Jew and Gentile are the same in this respect: they all have the same Lord who generously gives his riches to all those who ask him for them. Anyone who calls upon the name of the Lord will be saved.

Dear reader, can you remember a time when you asked Christ to come into your life? If you are uncertain, how about settling that issue right now? Do you believe that Christ died for your sins? Do you believe He rose from the dead to give you eternal life? Would you be willing to confess this truth to others? Do you want to call upon the name of the Lord right now? If that is your desire, do it this moment.

I don't know where you are reading this book. You might be completely alone or in a public place. If you are alone, I suggest you get down on your knees and pour out your heart to God in prayer. Tell Him about your hurts and pain. Confess your failure and need of a Savior. Invite Him to come into your heart and change your life. Thank Him for His love and concern for you. Of course, you can do all of this and not be on your knees. I am only suggesting this because it helps to lock in the experience as you bow before Almighty God. (If you would like to explore this further, check out "Jesus Will Help You!" at the end of this book.)

If you have a pen or pencil handy, write down the date in the margin of this book. You might say something like, "I received Christ into my heart today, Tuesday, March 25, 2001, at 2:30 P.M." This will be a wonderful reminder for you in the days ahead. Take a moment and do it now.

Another reason for poor choices may lie in the fact that you received Christ as your Savior, but He hasn't become Lord of your life. You may have been wandering and doing your own thing like the prodigal son did. You may have been overlooking or ignoring the still, small voice of God. Maybe you haven't been listening for the promptings of the Holy Spirit of God. Please, do not go a moment longer without running home to your Savior. He wants to help you change your life. His desire for you is that you experience His joy and peace. How long will you run from the Shepherd of heaven as He pursues His lost sheep?

The Bible uses a military term to describe turning to Jesus. The word is *repentance*. It simply means "about face." In the days of yore, if a military leader wanted his soldiers to march the opposite direction he would say, "Repent," and they would turn around. Do you need to repent and turn the opposite direction from which you have been going? Then do so today. Consider the following thoughts about repentance.

> Turn from your sins [repent]…turn to God…for the Kingdom of Heaven is coming soon (Matthew 3:2).

> So the disciples went out, telling everyone they met to turn from sin [repent] (Mark 6:12).

> Well, in the same way heaven will be happier over one lost sinner who returns [repents] to God than over ninety-nine others who haven't strayed away! (Luke 15:7).

> And Peter replied, "Each one of you must turn from sin [repent], return to God, and be baptized in the name of Jesus Christ for the forgiveness of your sins…" (Acts 2:38).

> Now change your mind and attitude to God and turn to him [repent] so he can cleanse away your sins and send you wonderful times of refreshment from the presence of the Lord and send Jesus your Messiah back to you again (Acts 3:19,20).

Receiving Christ as your personal Savior and repenting from your sins is the starting place for learning to make good choices. Being honest with God about your needs is the starting place for growth.

Repentance is a hearty sorrow for our past misdeeds, and is a sincere resolution and endeavor, to the utmost of our power, to conform all our actions to the law of God. It does not consist in one single act of sorrow, but in doing works meet for repentance; in a sincere obedience to the law of Christ for the remainder of our lives.

John Locke

Taking Action

Choice Evaluation

Take a few moments and review the following topics that represent areas of choice each of us face. Sometimes we make good choices; sometimes we make bad choices. All our decisions have results or consequences. On the line following the choice, jot down the situation and the decision you made. Then write down what the result was. When you are done, review your answers. Do your results indicate a pattern? Are you happy with it? Do you want to change it?

Area of Choice	*Results or Consequences*
Amount of sleep	Situation/Decision:
	Result:
Appearance	Situation/Decision:
	Result:
Attitude	Situation/Decision:
	Result:
Being alone	Situation/Decision:
	Result:
Career	Situation/Decision:
	Result:
Children	Situation/Decision:
	Result:

Chores   Situation/Decision:

                                Result:

Church   Situation/Decision:

                                Result:

Complaining   Situation/Decision:

                                Result:

Control of emotions   Situation/Decision:

                                Result:

Credit cards   Situation/Decision:

                                Result:

Discipline   Situation/Decision:

                                Result:

Drinking   Situation/Decision:

                                Result:

Eating   Situation/Decision:

                                Result:

Education   Situation/Decision:

                                Result:

Encouragement of others   Situation/Decision:

                                Result:

Exercise   Situation/Decision:

                                Result:

Friendliness   Situation/Decision:

                                Result:

Giving to others   Situation/Decision:

                                Result:

Goals   Situation/Decision:

                                Result:

Hobby

Situation/Decision:

Result:

Honesty

Situation/Decision:

Result:

Impulsiveness

Situation/Decision:

Result:

Indecision

Situation/Decision:

Result:

Jealousy

Situation/Decision:

Result:

Keeping promises

Situation/Decision:

Result:

Listening to others

Situation/Decision:

Result:

Lying   Situation/Decision:

                             Result:

Making mistakes   Situation/Decision:

                             Result:

Manners   Situation/Decision:

                             Result:

Marriage partner   Situation/Decision:

                             Result:

Negative thinking   Situation/Decision:

                             Result:

Patience   Situation/Decision:

                             Result:

Perfectionism   Situation/Decision:

                             Result:

Posture   Situation/Decision:

                                 Result:

Pride   Situation/Decision:

                                 Result:

Procrastination   Situation/Decision:

                                 Result:

Promptness   Situation/Decision:

                                 Result:

Reading materials   Situation/Decision:

                                 Result:

Savings   Situation/Decision:

                                 Result:

Self-pity   Situation/Decision:

                                 Result:

Sense of humor   Situation/Decision:

                                  Result:

Sexual involvement   Situation/Decision:

                                  Result:

Shyness   Situation/Decision:

                                  Result:

Smiling   Situation/Decision:

                                  Result:

Spare time   Situation/Decision:

                                  Result:

Spiritual life   Situation/Decision:

                                  Result:

Television   Situation/Decision:

                                  Result:

Temper   Situation/Decision:

                        Result:

Unforgiveness   Situation/Decision:

                        Result:

Vacation   Situation/Decision:

                        Result:

Worry   Situation/Decision:

                        Result:

Dear God,

I realize I have not been making choices that bring positive results. The pattern of my life has not been forming in the right way. Frankly, I'm tired of living this way. I want to change. I want to be a different person.

Please help me change. I have tried to do it on my own and have fallen flat on my face over and over again. I need Your strength. I need Your encouragement. I need hope that it is possible to change. I'm going to take a step of faith and thank You for Your answer, even though I don't see it yet. I'm in Your hands. Amen.

Dealing with Anger Changes Your Thinking

7

A wise man restrains his anger and overlooks insults. This is to his credit.

Proverbs 19:11

HAVE YOU EVER BEEN IN A FIGHT? I don't mean a verbal argument; I mean a physical fight with fists flying and punches being given and received. I have, and I must confess that it is not much fun. On one particular day I could tell I was just seconds away from being hit.

It began when I was walking across the summer camp I oversee and noticed a younger boy around 12 years of age. He was walking around our fire truck, looking at it. Soon he picked up the fire-hose nozzles and began to walk into the woods with them. I followed and watched as he tossed them into the forest. He did not see me as I picked up the nozzles. I then followed him to his cabin.

With the nozzles in my hands, I introduced myself to his mother and related the behavior of her son. The boy's father saw me talking with the mother. He came over to where we were standing. I shared with both of them what their son had done and the danger that he might have caused by stealing the nozzles.

The father immediately became angry. He whipped off his belt and began to spank his son right in front of me. He then turned to me and said, "Get the hell out of here!" He stormed off, leaving me standing with his wife.

I said, "I am sorry for all this trouble, but I thought you would want to know about your son's behavior." To which the wife replied, "You had better leave. Don is really mad. Here he comes again. You had better go."

As I turned to leave I was confronted by the physical presence of Don. I could tell he wanted to hit me. His face was red, his neck muscles were tight, and his fists were tightly clenched. Being trained in the martial arts, I knew that a blow was about to erupt in my direction.

"Go ahead and hit me if you like," I said. "I have dealt as fairly and honestly with you as I know how." My words startled Don. They made him pause for a moment. I continued to speak to him in a firm tone. My verbal comments prevented physical violence. We parted company with Don still angry and some issues unresolved, but a fist fight was avoided.

Anger is a universal emotion—everyone experiences it. Sometimes we are the ones who are angry; sometimes we are the recipients of other people's anger. Anger is a God-given emotion just like fear. Anger *and* fear are our friends if: our anger is toward injustice; our fear protects us from harm. However, anger and fear can become our enemies if we turn them toward hurting others or running from issues that need to be resolved. The negative aspects of anger are influenced by:

1. Our clouded and warped old sin nature
   - Basic selfishness

2. Our temperament and body chemistry
   - Our social and personality style (analytical, driving, amiable, expressive), along with things like low blood sugar and chemical imbalance

3. Personal desires, demands, and expectations
   - To meet our needs

4. Positive and negative modeling from our family of origin
   - Parents and relatives who were examples

5. Positive and negative personal experiences and interpersonal relationships
   - Watching others around us and our interaction with them

6. Uncontrolled outside forces
   - Accident, illness, natural disaster, loss

Anger can express itself actively or passively. Active forms include criticism, sarcasm, and ridicule. Some people seem to get pleasure from putting other people down. They say things like: "Is that your head—or did your body blow a bubble?" "I don't recall your face—but your breath is familiar."

Psychologists tell us that there are three reasons why we criticize others. First, we criticize the very things we are guilty of doing ourselves. Second, we criticize because we are unhappy about something, and we want others to join us in our unhappiness (the misery loves company syndrome).

Third, we criticize in order to elevate ourselves by lowering the character of others. Will Durant said, "To speak ill of others is a dishonest way of praising ourselves."

There's not the least thing can be said or done, but people will talk and find fault.

Miguel de Cervantes

The active forms of anger can become more severe through gossip, humiliation, and slander. These forms seek to destroy the reputation of others. Anger is also revealed through physical acts of bullying, beating others up, and even murder. Suicide is also an extreme act of anger; the individuals becomes angry enough to kill. They murder themselves.

The more "popular" forms of anger take on passive expressions. This includes silence. Nothing is quite so powerful and hurtful as shutting off communication with others. The Amish use "shunning" as a way to control the behavior of others. Silence will destroy a relationship quicker than any other method.

Many people who are upset do not like to admit they are angry. To express their emotions they use words such as: annoyed, irritated, frustrated, and exasperated. I used to have a friend who would pound the table with his fist and yell, "I am not mad! I am not mad! I am not mad!" Even though he said he was not mad, no one around agreed with him. His actions and body language told a different story. Deep-seated anger involves the concepts of disgust, repulsion, resentment, bitterness, and hatred. It is possible to smile and act cordial and still be filled with malice.

Studies at Columbia University in New York and Oregon State University reveal that under ordinary circumstances the average man loses his temper six times a week. Women under the same conditions lose their temper only three times a week. Research indicates that men are more likely to become angry over inanimate objects. They will throw the screwdriver across the garage or pound a wall. Women, on the other hand, generally get angry at other people because of real or imagined slights. Neither sex has patience for the other's methodology. Men can't understand why women get so upset over relationships, and women can't understand how men can get so angry at inanimate objects.

When you see a married couple coming down the street, the one who is two or three steps ahead is the one that's mad.

Helen Rowland

Anger is a strong component in the emotion of depression. It is possible to be angry without being depressed, but it is not possible to be depressed without being angry. In our counseling center I had an intake form that asked the question, "What is your sleep pattern like?" A classic sign of depression is a change in sleep patterns. The person has little or restless sleep or sleeps an abundant amount of time. This questioning process asks, "What is your sleep pattern like?" "Have you been encountering depression?" "Are you aware of anger directed at some individual or a circumstance that is difficult?" "Is there some hurt or loss that has come into your life?" Often anger is the key that leads us to the hurt or loss that has not been dealt with or resolved.

Are you an angry person? Do you display your anger in an active way or a passive way? Or have you become an expert in displaying your anger in both active and passive forms?

Learning to deal with anger takes two basic tracks. The first is dealing with anger *before* you become angry. The second is dealing with anger *after* you have become angry. Dealing with anger before you become angry is preventative maintenance. It is learning how to identify and stop anger before it takes control. Listed below are warning signs that indicate you may be dealing with some anger in your life. Place a check alongside any of the physical indicators you experience.

Physical Signs of Anger

- Accident proneness
- Asthma, hay fever
- Bladder problems
- Chest pains
- Constipation
- Diarrhea
- Heart problems
- Low back pain
- Migraine headaches
- Nausea and vomiting
- Neck pain
- Nervous stomach
- Overeating
- Runny nose
- Skin rashes (hives, eczema)
- Starvation
- Stuttering
- Tension headaches
- Throat problems
- Twitches
- Ulcers
- Upset stomach

Factors that Influence Anger

Place a check beside the ones that may be active in your experience.

- ❐ Boredom
- ❐ Criticism
- ❐ Damaged love affair
- ❐ Drugs and/or alcohol
- ❐ Envy
- ❐ Expectations for others
- ❐ Family environment
- ❐ Fear of failure
- ❐ Feelings of helplessness
- ❐ Feelings of rejection
- ❐ Feelings of uselessness
- ❐ Frustration
- ❐ General stress
- ❐ Humiliation or embarassment
- ❐ Ill health
- ❐ Injustice
- ❐ Insecurity
- ❐ Jealousy
- ❐ Lack of privacy
- ❐ Loss of goals
- ❐ Loss of job
- ❐ Loss of loved one through death
- ❐ Loss of respect
- ❐ Loss of sleep
- ❐ Mood swings
- ❐ Need for space
- ❐ Past experiences
- ❐ Perception and interpretation of situation
- ❐ Physical injury or handicap
- ❐ Religious background
- ❐ Revenge
- ❐ Selfishness
- ❐ Social pressure
- ❐ Temperament
- ❐ Weather

Anger has the power to control your thinking process unless you keep it in check. If you are angry with someone or something, it can become an obsession. Anger can keep you up at night. It can ruin your health and destroy your relationships. Anger can cost you your job. Anger can become a way of life for some people.

Do you get angry in certain locations? Do you get angry with selected individuals? Are there specific situations that trigger your anger? Take a moment and measure your anger with the following Anger Inventory. Answer each question by giving a rating from 0 to 4. This is a very general chart, so mark how you *usually* respond in tense situations. At the end of the inventory, total your score to get some idea of your involvement with anger. Be sure to answer honestly.

Anger Inventory

0—I would feel very little or no annoyance.

1—I would feel a little irritated.

2—I would feel moderately upset.

3—I would feel quite angry.

4—I would feel very angry.

---

1. Anger with my parents.   0 1 2 3 4

2. Anger with my brothers.   0 1 2 3 4

3. Anger with my sisters.   0 1 2 3 4

4. Anger with my children.   0 1 2 3 4

5. Anger with my spouse/boyfriend/
   girlfriend.   0 1 2 3 4

6. Anger with my in-laws.   0 1 2 3 4

7. Anger with my current friends.   0 1 2 3 4

8. Anger with my former friends.   0 1 2 3 4

9. Anger with my neighbors.   0 1 2 3 4

10. Anger with teachers.   0 1 2 3 4

11. Anger with bosses.   0 1 2 3 4

12. Anger with police.   0 1 2 3 4

13. Anger with government workers.   0 1 2 3 4

14. Anger with peers at work.   0 1 2 3 4

15. Anger with subordinates at work.   0 1 2 3 4

16. Anger with customers.   0 1 2 3 4

17. Anger with clients.   0 1 2 3 4

18. Anger with salespeople.   0 1 2 3 4

19. Anger with politicians.   0 1 2 3 4

20. Anger with religious leaders.   0 1 2 3 4

21. Anger with God.   0 1 2 3 4

22. Anger with strangers.   0 1 2 3 4

23. Anger with myself.   0 1 2 3 4

24. Anger with waiting in line.   0 1 2 3 4

25. Anger with traffic.   0 1 2 3 4

26. Anger with inanimate objects.   0 1 2 3 4

27. Anger with being overlooked.   0 1 2 3 4

28. Anger with being overcharged.   0 1 2 3 4

29. Anger with being blamed for
    something you didn't do.   0 1 2 3 4

30. Anger with being made fun of.   0 1 2 3 4

Take a moment and add up your score to get some idea of where you are on the Anger Inventory. The lowest possible score you could get on this inventory is zero. If that happened, you either misunderstood the inventory, weren't honest, or are superhuman. The highest score you could get is 120. If you registered this high, you are a walking volcano ready to erupt on anyone in any situation.

0–20   The anger you are experiencing is remarkably low. A very low percent of the population will score this way. You are one of the select few.

21–40   You are substantially more peaceful than the average person.

41–60   You are responding to life's annoyances with an average amount of anger.

61–80   You frequently react in an angry way to life's annoyances. You are substantially more irritable than the average person.

80–120   You win the prize for anger. You are plagued by frequent, intense, and furious reactions that do not quickly disappear. You may be harboring negative feelings long after the initial incident has passed. You may have a reputation for exploding on others. Your blood pressure could be high and you may be experiencing frequent tension headaches. Your hostile outbursts may be getting you into trouble and damaging relationships. Your anger could be causing much trouble for you at home and at work. Only a small percent of the adult population react as intensely as you do.

Anger is a common experience to everyone, although some people struggle with it more than others. Very seldom does anger solve a problem or make a situation better. In rare cases, righteous indignation has ended child abuse, spousal beatings, and other social problems; however, this is the exception, not the rule. Most of the anger we experience or are the recipients of has negative consequences.

**Anyone can become angry—that is easy,
but to be angry with the right person,
to the right degree, at the right time,
for the right purpose, and in the right way—
this is not easy.**
Aristotle

Anger makes difficult situations worse. It sparks aggression, creates health problems, and deepens depression. Anger is a strong component that results in divorce, anxiety, guilt, and suicide. Anger causes much personal distress and uses up much of our thinking time. It can cost a person his job. Anger has been the cause for damaged property as individuals have physically expressed their hostility. Many people have lost their lives when deep-seated anger turned to murder. Can you remember situations where your angry outbursts caused personal embarrassment? In general, have your anger expressions helped or damaged your relationships? How many people have hurt you by their angry comments? How many relationships have been terminated by anger?

To help you get a handle on the emotion of anger, it would be good to keep an "Anger Diary." For the next three weeks, write down any incidents of anger that you experience. It is important that the diary include:

1. The time of the angry experience.

2. The place where it occurred.

3. The circumstances surrounding the experience.

4. The people involved.

5. Your actual response at the time. (Did you withdraw? Did you attack?)

6. The amount of time you spent thinking about the situation after it was over.

7. The thoughts you had about the event after it was over.

After keeping the "Anger Diary" for three weeks, review its contents. Is there a recurring theme or topic? Is your anger directed at, or involved with, particular individuals? Does your anger occur at a certain time of day or express itself at a particular place? Do you have a consistent response to anger by either attacking or withdrawing? Do you spend an inordinate amount of time and unnecessary emotions thinking about anger-producing situations?

The first step in getting a handle on anger is to understand what is triggering it in your life. Gaining insight and understanding in this area helps you become fully responsible for all of your actions and thoughts. This creates hope for change, which stimulates motivation, which causes thinking and behavior change, which brings about peace and a sense of well-being.

To become proficient in the area of anger management, it is important to understand the anger process. It is comprised of the event that triggers the anger, our mental responses, our verbal responses, and our physical responses.

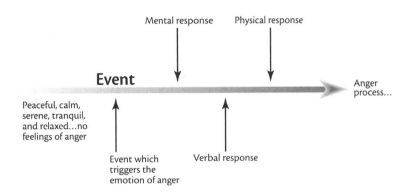

The event is the trigger that sets off the emotion of anger. It could be that you are late for an appointment and there is slow traffic in front of you. It might be that your spouse makes a comment that hurts you. You may have just spilled something on your clothes or ripped your jacket on a nail. A life event has occurred that you don't like and has caused you irritation.

Mental Response

When one of these life events occurs, it is helpful to follow the steps below. They will help you control your emotions and reduce your anger.

1. *Get more information before you respond.* It is possible that you may have misunderstood what was said or you have

misinterpreted the situation. This happened to me in Siberia when a ministry I am involved in presented a seminar on leadership to military leaders. At one point while I was speaking I realized the audience had been sitting for a long period of time, and it might be good to have them stand and stretch. I said, "Will you please stand for a moment?" This was translated and one of the generals immediately got angry and said, "You can't tell me to stand! You're not a general!" I was taken aback by his response. He had clearly misunderstood and responded in anger. I was about to clarify my request when the situation was taken care of by one of the generals on our speaking team.

In Proverbs 18:13, wise King Solomon said, "He who answers before listening—that is his folly and his shame" (NIV). It is important to get all the facts before we get our emotions involved and respond to others. Sometimes it is helpful to ask questions like: "Could you clarify what you meant?" "I am not sure if I quite understood you, could you rephrase your comment?" "Would you please help me understand what you meant by _____?"

2. *Go to the memory file.* Ask yourself if you are getting feelings of anger because of what the person is saying or because this person brings to mind someone else.

Maybe he or she reminds you of a teacher you once had that you didn't like. The individual might be speaking in a tone of voice that reminds you of your mother, father, or some other authority figure in your life. Before you respond, be sure you are not dredging up past experiences and loading them onto the person or situation you are presently facing.

3. *Watch out for displaced anger.* You might have had a bad day at work and were yelled at by your supervisor. Then, when you get home, you find that your son left his bicycle laying on

the walkway coming into the house. Do you yell at him? Would you normally yell at your son for such an event? Or are you yelling because you are still upset with your supervisor? Is your lack of patience due to other issues in your life you are dealing with? If this happens, ask God to help you deal with the *real* cause of anger, rather than venting your emotions on innocent bystanders.

4. *Evaluate your angry feelings.* What is causing you to feel the way you do? Did someone say something to hurt you? Were you passed over by someone? Have you experienced some type of loss? Were you embarrassed? Are you dealing with feelings of guilt for something you said or did? Are you feeling threatened? Is there too much change going on in your life at this time?

5. *Remind yourself that God is in control.* Nothing catches God off guard. He is not surprised by the events in your life:

> We can rejoice, too, when we run into problems and trials, for we know that they are good for us—they help us learn to be patient. And patience develops strength of character in us and helps us trust God more each time we use it until finally our hope and faith are strong and steady. Then, when that happens, we are able to hold our heads high no matter what happens and know that all is well, for we know how dearly God loves us, and we feel this warm love everywhere within us because God has given us the Holy Spirit to fill our hearts with his love (Romans 5:3-5).

6. *Share your anger with God.* Often King David shared his anger, frustration, and depression with God. The psalms are filled with David's expressions of strong emotion. Some of these feelings are picked up in Psalm 39:1-4:

I said, "I will watch my ways and keep my tongue from sin; I will put a muzzle on my mouth as long as the wicked are in my presence." But when I was silent and still, not even saying anything good; my anguish increased. My heart grew hot within me, and as I meditated, the fire burned; then I spoke with my tongue: "Show me, O LORD, my life's end and the number of my days; let me know how fleeting is my life" (NIV).

7. *Face the sin of your anger.* Don't pass the buck; don't blame someone else for your anger. Own it, face it, and take responsibility for it. Confess your angry thoughts to God. Ask *Him* to take away the angry habit patterns that have made a deep rut in your life. Forgive those who have hurt you or have injured you in some fashion. Thank God for bringing situations into your life that help you develop patience and grow more Christlike. Think about positive things; do not dwell on past hurts and losses.

Verbal Response

1. *Discipline your mind.* Think about what you are going to say *before* you open your mouth and start talking. Formulate the conflicting issue clearly. As you express your thoughts, do not attack the individual with put-downs and harsh words. Attack words do not solve a conflict; they increase it and lock it in.

2. *Don't hold things in for long periods of time.* Often people hold in their hurts and frustrations until they develop into full-blown anger. Instead of dealing with a wastebasket of problems, some people back up a whole dump truck and unload it on the individual they are upset with. No one can

deal with that much garbage at once. Remember how to eat an elephant? You eat it one bite at a time. The same is true of problems. Deal with them one at a time.

3. *Don't withdraw into silence.* Nothing destroys a relationship quicker than silence. Not talking to each other destroys friendships. Shakespeare said, "Go oft to the house of your friend for weeds soon choke an unused path." Silence begins when someone has been hurt and withdraws. He or she does not want to be hurt anymore. This is understandable, but it does not solve the problem or reconcile the relationship. It is not easy to crawl out of the cave of silence, but it is absolutely essential if there is to be a restoration with the person who hurt you. You need to rise above the conflict and become the reconciler. God will help you do this.

4. *Be open to correction and criticism.* No one likes to be corrected or criticized. No one wants to be forced to admit they are wrong. It is at this point that people want to argue that someone has hurt them, so they are victims. This very well may be true, but how are you responding to that hurt? You are not responsible for what others do. You are responsible for your reaction to what the person has done. Has your reaction been godly? Have you been responding as Jesus would respond if He were in the same situation?

5. *Share one issue at a time.* When it comes to discussing your hurt or frustration with another individual, deal with only one issue at a time. Don't get sidetracked; stick to the discussion at hand until it is resolved. Don't overload the situation.

6. *Don't use the past against people.* Have you heard about the man who came running into the counselor's office? He said, "You've got to help me, my wife's historical!" "You mean

hysterical," said the counselor. "No," said the man, "I mean historical. She keeps bringing up the past." The reason people bring up the past is to hurt the person who has hurt them. It is a form of revenge and guilt used to control and punish those with whom they have a conflict.

7. *Share your expectations.* One of the major problems in relationships is that people do not share their expectations. Somehow, we think the other person has a crystal ball that will help them know how we are feeling or the way we want to be treated. Not only is this unfair to others, it is not even logical. We only see other people's actions and behaviors; we are not capable of truly understanding their motivations unless they communicate clearly with us. And other people can't understand us unless we also communicate effectively.

8. *State your hurt or complaint objectively.* When you get to the place where you are sharing your hurts or complaints, do it in such a manner that the other person can understand you. Don't let your emotions get out of hand. Deal with the issues in a calm, logical manner.

9. *Share your hurt or complaint in private.* The kindest thing is to talk to the other person in private. People don't like to be reprimanded in public or have their "dirty laundry" hung for all to see. Jesus said, "If your brother sins against you, go and show him his fault, just between the two of you. If he listens to you, you have won your brother over" (Matthew 18:15 NIV).

10. *Don't make threats to terminate or leave the relationship.* Never precipitate a crisis unless you are willing to face the music and go through with it. Making threats is not a game

to see who can control the other person. You may have thoughts of terminating the relationship, but do not express those thoughts in words. Don't use this "power play" to get the other person to conform to your demands. It will turn around and bite you in the rear end. Making threats to terminate a relationship is an attempt to hurt the other person. It can also cause a great rift in trust.

11. *Don't exaggerate.* State your issues and concerns fairly and truthfully. Don't embellish them or make them bigger than they are. Exaggeration can be used as another form of punishment or guilt. It does not help solve the problem, it only increases it.

12. *Allow for reaction time.* You have had the advantage of thinking about the problem for a period of time. If you press for an answer before the individual has thought the matter through, you may regret it. The other person may respond in the way you want and then not follow through because he or she is not truly committed to the immediate choice. People get angry when forced into a decision with their backs to the wall. Respect them enough to give them time to think the matter through.

13. *Look for a solution.* Honestly ask yourself, "Am I looking for revenge or am I looking for a solution?" Looking for solutions is the responsible way to manage anger.

Physical Response

I have been asked if it is ever right to respond with anger physically. The answer is no—except for extremely rare occasions. This might occur when your family is being attacked or your nation is threatened by an enemy. I have only had this experience once. It occurred in Los Banos, California.

My daughter and I were walking across a large parking lot when several teenagers in a car tried to run us down. I just barely had enough time to move my daughter out of the way before the car reached us. I reacted in anger by kicking the door of the car as they drove by. They stopped the car about 50 feet ahead of us and the doors flew open. They were going to get out and finish the job. I had a different idea in mind. I ran toward their car as fast as I could. I didn't care how many there were in the car. They had just attacked my family with a large, deadly weapon. The kids changed their minds and barely got the car in gear by the time I got to the driver's side of the car. They sped off and yelled swear words out the window. This was one of those rare times when it was right to get angry physically.

Most other physical anger takes place because the individuals don't have the communication skills to deal with the problem verbally or mentally. People who inflict physical injury on others are trying to control situations that have gotten out of hand for them. They do it in the only way they know how...with violence. They may also be motivated by desires to hurt the other person, get revenge, or simply to let them know who is boss. Whatever the motivation is, it brings devastation to relationships and increases the problem.

If you are dealing with anger in a physical manner, you are in need of immediate help. Admit you have a problem and seek assistance before someone is physically harmed, emotionally damaged, or killed because of your temper. This is not a situation where you can say, "I'll work out the problem myself." Be courageous enough to seek help.

**Whenever you are angry, be assured
that it is not only a present evil,
but that you have increased the habit.**

Epictetus

Dear God,

It is so easy for me to get angry. I'm impatient and often want people to immediately respond to my needs. I struggle with this emotion when people cut in line, I'm in slow traffic, and a host of other situations.

Holding grudges and having strong desires to get even with those who have hurt me or taken advantage of me are nothing new. Sometimes I just clam up and don't want to talk. Other times I let my venom out on others…usually the people in my own family.

Lord, I'm tired of being angry. I'm tired of holding resentments. I'm tired of feeling alone. How desperately I need You to come to my aid and help me tame the tiger of anger. Help me take responsibility for my thoughts and actions. Amen.

Forgiveness
Can Become
the Road to Health

8

*Everyone says forgiveness is a lovely idea, until
they have something to forgive.*

C.S. Lewis

I HATE YOU; I HATE YOU," I used to say to my brother. To which my mother would reply, "Now, Robert, don't say that you hate your brother. You can say you dislike him but never say that you hate him."

Well, the fact of the matter was that I hated my brother. I thought he was mean to me. When he hog-tied me in the backyard and left me tied up all afternoon, I thought that was mean. When he and his friends would hold me down, pull up my shirt, and rub grass all over me to make me itch, I thought that was mean. When they buried me up to my waist in the backyard and left me there, I thought that was mean. I longed for the day I could beat my brother up. I longed for the day I could get revenge for all of his meanness.

Have you ever been hurt by someone and wanted to get even? Have you ever felt that what was happening to you was not fair? You may have come from a dysfunctional home where you had an alcoholic parent. You may have a parent or relative that was physically, emotionally, or sexually abusive. You may have brothers or sisters you did not get along with, or coworkers who treated you unfairly or made fun of you. Maybe you now have an employer who is hardnosed and difficult to get along with. Or maybe your marriage is filled with hostility and anger. You may have been the victim of a robbery, assault, or rape. A member of your family may have been killed by a drunk driver. You may have lost money in the stock market or lost money in a "sure thing" land investment.

There are many causes of hurt and loss in this life. There are no relationships that do not have tension at some point. You cannot live in a community of people without experiencing conflicts. In fact, in any human relationship you are exposed to the possibility of pain, injury, suffering, and alienation in some form.

There is a strong tendency in all of us to assign blame to the other person or event for all of our troubles. When we are hurt by others, whether it is in the form of yelling or silence, we avoid them. Sometimes we pretend there is no problem and revert to denial. Often we develop feelings of resentment toward those who have done us wrong.

As I mentioned, I longed for the day I could get even with my brother. Then one day the opportunity came. When I was older and much larger, my brother began to push me around and "wrestle" with me. Little did he know that he was tapping into 20 years of built-up ire. With the strength of my resentment and the desire for revenge, I threw my brother to the ground and injured him. It was then that I realized the hollowness of revenge. I felt terrible. I had dropped to his level...and perhaps then some. An old adage says, "If the other person injures you, you may forget the injury; but if you injure him, you will always remember."

The best manner of avenging ourselves is by not resembling him who has injured us.
Jane Porter

Resentment is created by the accumulation of unexpressed anger. It is one of the most destructive emotions in human relationships and can destroy personal well-being and emotional health. The definition of *resentment* comes from the concept "to feel strongly again." Resentment seems to give us power and control over others. We can use this emotion to avoid communication with those whom we do not like. We can use it like a shield to protect us from being hurt again in the future. The power of resentment can make others feel guilty for hurting us. It helps us avoid our true feelings about the hurtful event. Resentment justifies our "victim" status and keeps us believing that we are correct in our view of the matter. It can short-circuit our taking responsibility for our thoughts and behaviors. Resentment can develop into a deep grudge and extreme bitterness.

Unfortunately, resentment is like biting a dog after it has bitten you. Resentment eventually becomes its own executioner. It destroys us instead of the person we're mad at. Resentment is self-inflicted torture.

I remember a childhood event where a salesman in a variety store kicked me out of the store. I don't remember why he did it, but I was probably "horsing around" and he was justified in doing it. What I do remember is that I was very angry with him. I said to myself, *I will not enter that store as long as he works there.* This resentment built to the point where I didn't go into the store for seven years. No big deal, right? Wrong. It was a big deal to a little boy because it was the only candy store in the neighborhood. Who suffered the most by all this anger and resentment? It certainly was not the salesperson.

Don't carry a grudge. While you're carrying the grudge, the other guy's out dancing.

Buddy Hackett

Have you ever wondered why forgiveness is so difficult? It is because the injured party lets the person who has done the injury go free. Archibald Hart says it this way, "Forgiveness is surrendering my right to hurt you back if you hurt me." Mark Twain expressed this same concept when he stated, "Forgiveness is the fragrance the violet sheds on the heel that has crushed it."

Let's say that I came over to your house to visit. You invite me in, and we go into your living room. You say, "Please sit down." For some reason I choose not to sit in a big soft chair but instead sit down in a small rocking chair. Before you can speak, the small rocking chair collapses under my weight. You see, I did not know it was an antique rocking chair that had been handed down through your family. To you it was a "display" piece in your home. Everyone is in shock.

I say, "I'm sorry. Can I buy you another one?"

"No," you reply.

"Can I replace it?"

"No," you say with sadness and pain in your voice.

"Will you forgive me?"

Inside, you groan with pain.

Can you see why forgiveness is so difficult? The person who inflicts the injury goes free, leaving the injured party in pain and misery. This is a dirty deal, and it is not fair. It is not a pleasant experience in the least. Repayment for the offense is impossible. I cannot put the broken chair back into the same condition it was before the accident. Your trying to get revenge on me will not replace the chair. Resenting me for breaking the chair will not restore it. In forgiveness, the injured party has to make peace with the pain and accept the loss. This is why most people do not like to forgive—it's too painful and too costly.

The Nuts and Bolts of Forgiveness

Forgiveness is *not* the denying of the emotions of hurt and anger. Forgiveness *does not* repress and hold down feelings. Forgiveness *does not* suppress the fullness of the pain. Forgiveness *does not* pretend that everything is fine and act nice when there really is a problem.

Forgiveness *is* very realistic. Forgiveness *is* honest; it does not hide its head in the sand thinking that difficulties will go away if they're not acknowledged. Forgiveness does not occupy the fantasy that what is unchangeable can be changed or undone.

Forgiveness does not passively accept or condone unacceptable behavior. It does not rationalize, give alibis, or make excuses for the offending party. It is not a doormat for evil to continue unconfronted. Forgiveness is not afraid to exercise "tough love" and tell the truth. Forgiveness is not afraid to talk about repentance, restoration, and reconciliation. It is not an emotional umbilical cord that allows the offending party to avoid personal responsibility.

Forgiveness is not isolation from the person who has done the offending. It does not take the attitude of superiority or piously hand out pity to the offender. Forgiveness does not place blame or make the other person feel guilty.

The weak can never forgive;
forgiveness is the attribute of the strong.
Mahatma Gandhi

Forgiveness is commanded by God as an act of how we should live in harmony with others. It was illustrated when Christ died for our sins and let us go free:

> So, as those who have been chosen of God, holy and beloved, put on a heart of compassion, kindness, humility, gentleness, and patience; bearing with one another, and forgiving each other, whoever has a complaint against anyone; just as the Lord forgave you, so also should you (Colossians 3:12,13 NASB).

This passage clarifies the attitude of those who forgive others. They have compassion. They look at the offending party with new eyes. They seek to understand the other person's motivation and background. They remember that the offender is precious in the eyes of God. Catherine the Great, "Empress of Russia," said, "The more a man knows, the more he forgives." Those who forgive are kind. They do not seek revenge; they seek restoration and reconciliation. Although they have been hurt, they try not to hurt back but ask, "How would Jesus respond in this situation?" Hannah More said, "A Christian will find it cheaper to pardon than to resent. Forgiveness saves the expense of anger, the cost of hatred, and the waste of spirits."

Those who forgive are humble. They try not to lord the offense over the offending party or make the person feel guilty. Those who forgive are gentle. They speak the truth in love with a desire to help offenders face their responsibility and grow through the experience. Being gentle and kind are acts of great courage and strength. Being gentle is a choice. St. Francis de Sales said, "Nothing is so strong as gentleness; nothing so gentle as real strength."

Those who forgive are patient. Have you ever desired more patience? Patience comes from trouble. We do not need patience when everything is going our way; it is only when things are going against us that we need it. Those who forgive go through the experience of pain, hurt, and loss. It is during that time that they exercise patience toward the offending party which increases patience overall. It has been said that patience is a bitter plant that has sweet fruit.

Those who forgive bear with one another. This entails more than putting up with others and their behaviors. It means to carry the burden imposed by others without complaint. People who forgive let complaints roll off their backs. They endure the pain of the complaint and make a choice to ignore it. This is illustrated in Proverbs 19:11, which states: "A man's wisdom gives him patience; it is to his glory to overlook an offense" (NIV).

Forgiveness does not come by accident. It is a choice. It is an attitude. It is a process. It is a way of life. Forgiveness is not an emotion. If people had to wait until they felt like forgiving others, pigs would fly before it would happen.

Forgiveness is found in the will. It is a promise; it is a commitment to three things, as Jay E. Adams suggests:

1. I will not use the event against them in the future.

2. I will not talk to others about them.

3. I will not dwell on it myself.

Forgiveness does not beat the offending party over the head with their offense trying to make them feel guilty. It does not try to destroy the reputation of the offending party or get revenge by sharing the transgression with others. Forgiveness does not wallow in the misery of the conflict. It gets up and moves on with life. It does not rip off the scabs to see if the offense is healing because this only prolongs the hurt.

I had a friend who was speaking at a conference center during the summer. About halfway through the week a woman came to him for counsel. She began to pour out the story of her divorce and the difficulty she was experiencing trying to get over it. After about 20 minutes my friend said, "May I ask you a few questions?"

"Of course," said the woman.

"How long ago did your divorce occur?"

"About two years."

"How many people have you talked with this week about your divorce?"

"Including you?"

"Yes, including me."

The woman thought for a moment and said, "About six."

To which my friend responded, "You know, I think I, too, would have a hard time getting over my divorce if I talked to six people a week about it for two years."

Clara Barton, the founder of the American Red Cross, was once reminded of an especially cruel thing that had been done to her years before, but she seemed not to recall it. "Don't you remember it?" her friend asked. "No," came the reply. "I distinctly remember forgetting the incident."

**There is no point in burying the hatchet
if you're going to put up a marker on the site.**
Sydney Harris

Forgiveness has the courage to work through problems rather than ignoring them or pretending they are not there. Jesus addressed this in Matthew 18:15-17 (NASB):

> And if your brother sins, go and reprove him in private; if he listens to you, you have won your brother. But if he does not listen to you, take one or two more with you, so that by the mouth of two or three witnesses every fact may be confirmed. And if he refuses to listen to them, tell it to the church; and if he refuses to listen even to the church, let him be to you as a Gentile and a tax-gatherer.

What is the purpose of forgiveness? The act of forgiveness restores and reconciles broken relationships. What happens if one of the parties does not want to restore the relationship? Does forgiveness still take place? That is like asking, "Which comes first, the chicken or the egg?" Does forgiveness take place first and then repentance, or does repentance take place first and then forgiveness? To answer the first question—the chicken comes first. God does not lay any eggs. To answer the second question—forgiveness comes first, then repentance. Christ is our example in this. He forgives us our sins before we repent. The joy that forgiveness brings comes when we repent and turn from our sin. We can forgive others their offenses, but we both may not experience the joy of restoration and reconciliation until repentance of the offender occurs. Sometimes they do not repent, and we are left with a true but hollow forgiveness. That is a painful experience.

When you forgive someone and he or she does not repent, it hurts. In a very small way you experience how God feels when people will not turn from their sins and accept His forgiveness. The heart of God aches because of His love for them. He does not turn His back on them because of their rejection. He keeps reaching out with the desire that someday they will repent and run back into His arms. We should follow His example.

But what happens if the offender hurts us again after we have forgiven them? Jesus addresses this in Matthew 18:21,22 (NASB) in talking with Peter:

> Then Peter came and said to Him, "Lord, how often shall my brother sin against me and I forgive him? Up to seven times?" Jesus said to him, "I do not say to you, up to seven times, but up to seventy times seven."

Dear reader, how many times has God forgiven your transgressions? I have been asked, "What if the person I need to forgive has moved out of town, and I cannot locate him? What if the person I need to forgive has died?" Then I suggest that you do the same thing the Old Testament leaders did when they owed money to someone who died or moved away. They brought the money owed to the temple as an offering to God. They gave the obligation to the Lord. If you need to forgive someone who has passed away or cannot be found, bring your forgiveness to the Lord as an offering. Give it to Him.

The classic story in the Bible about forgiveness is the story of Joseph. As you will remember, Joseph's brothers were extremely jealous of him. At first they plotted to murder him, but then decided to sell him into slavery. While in slavery, Joseph worked for a man called Potiphar. Joseph tried to make the best of his unfortunate circumstance and worked very diligently as a servant. Potiphar put Joseph in charge of all the other house servants. Potiphar's wife was attracted to Joseph and tried to seduce him. Being a man of integrity, Joseph ran from the situation.

Potiphar's wife was angry at being rejected. She made up a story and told her husband that Joseph had attempted to rape her. After Potiphar cast him into prison, Joseph endeavored to make the best of being in prison. The warden of the prison eventually put Joseph in charge of all the other prisoners. While in prison, he helped two men, only asking that they endeavor to free him from prison. The "cupbearer of Pharoah" forgot about Joseph's request, and Joseph remained in prison for at least two years. Eventually, the cupbearer remembered Joseph, and he was brought before Pharoah. Through a set of circumstances, Joseph became the second of command under the Pharoah of Egypt.

Up to this point in Joseph's life, we learn several things of importance. The first is that Joseph faced many difficulties and was hurt greatly by those around him:

1. His brothers were jealous of him and hated him.

2. He was sold into slavery.

3. Potiphar's wife made up stories about him and slandered his reputation.

4. Potiphar threw him into prison.

5. The cupbearer forgot about him, and Joseph spent extra time in prison.

Joseph was treated unfairly: He lost his freedom; he lost his reputation; he lost his family. You would think that these experiences would make him angry and bitter. You would think he would long for revenge and get even with the people who had deliberately hurt him. But he did not.

Another thing we learn about Joseph was that he did not dwell on his misfortunes and wallow in his misery. He tried to overcome his circumstances by being diligent in his work. He took all the lemons in his life and made lemonade. There is nothing like good, hard work to get our minds off our troubles.

One pardons to the degree that one loves.

La Rochefoucauld

The third thing we learn about Joseph was that he was a man who was filled with forgiveness. This is seen when his brothers came to Egypt to buy food for their family. The brothers do not recognize Joseph, but Joseph recognized his brothers. He now has the perfect opportunity to get even, but he chooses instead to forgive. This wonderful story is found in Genesis chapters 37 to 50. At one point in the story, Joseph reveals himself to his brothers:

> Then Joseph could no longer control himself before all his attendants, and he cried out, "Have everyone leave my presence!" So there was no one with Joseph when he made himself known to his brothers. And he wept so loudly that the Egyptians heard him, and Pharoah's household heard about it. Then Joseph said to his brothers, "I am Joseph! Is my father still living?"

But his brothers were not able to answer him, because they were terrified at his presence.

Then Joseph said to his brothers, "Come close to me." When they had done so, he said, "I am your brother Joseph, the one you sold into Egypt! And now, do not be distressed and do not be angry with yourselves for selling me here, because it was to save lives that God sent me ahead of you. For two years now there has been famine in the land, and for the next five years there will not be plowing and reaping. But God sent me ahead of you to preserve for you a remnant on earth and to save your lives by a great deliverance. So then, it was not you who sent me here, but God" (Genesis 45:1-8 NIV).

The fourth quality we learn about Joseph was that he did not make his brothers feel guilty for their ill treatment of him. He did not demand any form of repayment for their offense.

The next thing we discover is that Joseph saw the big picture regarding the problems in his life. He knew God was in control, and He was not surprised at all the difficulties Joseph faced. He realized that God had something for him to learn from the pain and misery. Joseph trusted God; he believed that all of the events in his life would eventually bring God glory. Joseph worked through his problems by faith.

The sixth thing about Joseph was that he was very gracious, kind, and gentle. This is seen when Joseph's father passed away. His brothers thought Joseph was just being nice because the father was living. Now that their father was dead they feared Joseph would exercise his revenge and retaliation—that's what they would have done.

When Joseph's brothers saw that their father was dead, they said, "What if Joseph holds a grudge against us and pays us back for all the wrongs we did to him?" So they sent word to Joseph, saying, "Your father left these instructions before he died [of course this was a lie from his brothers]: 'This is what you are to say to Joseph: I ask you to forgive your brothers the sins and the wrongs they committed in treating you so badly.' Now please forgive the sins of the servants of the God of your father." When their message came to him, Joseph wept.

His brothers then came and threw themselves down before him. "We are your slaves," they said.

But Joseph said to them, "Don't be afraid. Am I in the place of God? You intended to harm me, but God intended it for good to accomplish what is now being done, the saving of many lives. So then, don't be afraid. I will provide for you and your children." And he reassured them and spoke kindly to them (Genesis 50:15-21 NIV).

Dear reader, please reread the life of Joseph and ask yourself, "What lessons does God want to teach me through the example of Joseph?" My prayer for you is that you may realize that the difficult situations you face, the harm brought on by others, can be used by God to help you grow and influence the lives of others.

Praise be to the God and Father of our Lord Jesus Christ, the Father of compassion and the God of all comfort, who comforts us in all our troubles, so that we can comfort those in trouble with the comfort we ourselves have received from God. For just as the sufferings of Christ flow over into our lives, so also through Christ our comfort overflows. If we are distressed, it is for your comfort and salvation; if we are comforted, it is for your comfort, which produces in you patient endurance of the same sufferings we suffer. And our hope for you is firm, because we know that just as you share in our sufferings, so also you share in our comfort (2 Corinthians 1:3-7 NIV).

Sometimes we find it hard to forgive. We forget that forgiveness is as much for us as for the other person. If you can't forgive it's like holding a hot coal in your hand— you're the one getting burned...

Jennifer James

Dear God,

You are going to have to help me. I have been carrying hurt and anger so long that I don't have the strength to lift it off my back. I have been wallowing in the muddy swamp of resentment, and I don't know how to climb out. I have tried, but I keep sliding back in.

Please send a rescue team immediately! Also send a big water truck of forgiveness to wash away the pain and self-pity that has covered my life. I would like to get cleaned up so that I can be used by You, to help others who are in the swamp. Amen.

Giving to Others Makes Us Mature

9

No person was ever honored for what he received. Honor has been the reward for what he gave.

Calvin Coolidge

Dr. Karl Menninger, the famous psychiatrist who founded the Menninger Clinic, was one day asked how to prevent a nervous breakdown from coming on. He suggested that the best way would be to pull down all the shades in your house, turn off all of the lights, lock all of the doors, and "go across the railroad tracks and find someone in need and do something for him."

It is easy to become so focused on our own problems and trials that we do not see the needs of others around us. Often in our search for contentment we forget that happiness is like a butterfly. If we try to catch the butterfly, it flies away. But when we busy ourselves with doing other tasks, the butterfly of happiness comes and lands on our shoulders. When we help others, we will find that our troubles disappear and delight lands in our life. The great Dr. Albert Schweitzer said, "One thing I know: The only ones among you who will be really happy are those who will have sought and found how to serve." We can serve by giving our money, time, and talents.

I am reminded of these words from Jesus Christ: "It is more blessed to give than to receive" (Acts 20:35). How are you doing in the area of giving and serving? Paul, the apostle, addressed this concept in Galatians 6:7-10 (NIV):

> Do not be deceived: God cannot be mocked. A man reaps what he sows. The one who sows to please his sinful nature, from that nature will reap destruction; the one who sows to please the Spirit, from the Spirit will reap eternal life. Let us not become weary in doing good for at the proper time we will reap a harvest if we do not give up. Therefore, as we have opportunity, let us do good to all people, especially to those who belong to the family of believers.

When it comes to giving money, we are told in 2 Corinthians 9:6-15 (NIV):

> Remember this: Whoever sows sparingly will also reap sparingly, and whoever sows generously will also reap generously. Each man should give what he has decided in his heart to give, not reluctantly or under compulsion, for God loves a cheerful giver. And God is able to make all grace abound to you, so that in all things at all times, having all that you need, you will abound in every good work. As it is written: "He has scattered abroad his gifts to the poor; his righteousness endures forever."
>
> Now he who supplies seed to the sower and bread for food will also supply and increase your store of seed and will enlarge the harvest of your righteousness.

> You will be made rich in every way so that you can be generous on every occasion, and through us your generosity will result in thanksgiving to God.
>
> This service that you perform is not only supplying the needs of God's people but is also overflowing in many expressions of thanks to God. Because of the service by which you have proved yourselves, men will praise God for the obedience that accompanies your confession of the gospel of Christ, and for your generosity in sharing with them and with everyone else. And in their prayers for you their hearts will go out to you, because of the surpassing grace God has given you. Thanks be to God for his indescribable gift!

Let's talk about giving for a minute. I am not suggesting you give to a particular organization, school, or charity. I am talking about developing an attitude of gratefulness and thankfulness that displays itself by a giving heart. Winston Churchill said, "We make a living by what we get, but we make a life by what we give." There are always people who are less fortunate than you or I. Do you care about them? Have you received good things from the Creator that you could share with others?

Rest assured that if you cannot be generous with a meager income, you will never be generous when you become wealthy. I have heard many people say that if they were rich they would give money away to help others. My question is, Why don't you start now? Habits start with small repeated actions. A giving heart is developed by giving what you can on a continuous basis. I had a very close friend who said, "Do your giving while you're living, so you're knowing where it's going."

Proverbs 11:24,25 (NIV) says "One man gives freely, yet gains even more; another withholds unduly, but comes to poverty. A generous man will prosper; he who refreshes others will himself be refreshed." There is one pleasure that human beings never tire of, and that is the joy that comes from helping someone who really needs us. Robert South stated it this way: "If there be any truer measure of a man than what he does, it must be by what he gives." Jackie Robinson said, "A life isn't significant except for its impact on other lives." Victor Hugo captured the thought when he said, "As the purse is emptied, the heart is filled."

**Money giving is a very good criterion
of a person's mental health.
Generous people are rarely
mentally ill people.**

Karl Menninger

Giving follows the law of sowing. A farmer sows seed into the soil. In due time the seeds blossom, produce fruit, and feed many (including the farmer). What can we learn from the farmer? We can't reap until we sow, nor will we experience the joy of giving until we do it. The seeds must have time to germinate. We can't dig up the seeds every other day to see how they are growing. We may not see immediate results from our giving but over time they will bear fruit. The more seeds we sow the more fruit will be produced. The more we develop the habit of giving, the more others will be helped. As our wealth increases, so does our ability to help people. As we learn to give, we receive more than financial dividends from our gifts.

No one can force us to give. It has to come from a sincere desire to help others as we have been helped. Seneca said, "He that does good to another does good also to himself, not only in the consequence, but in the very act. For the consciousness of well-doing is in itself ample reward."

**The greatest pleasure I know
is to do a good action by stealth,
and have it found out by accident.**

Charles Lamb

One Christmas, my wife and I decided we wanted to teach our children the joy of giving. I contacted the minister at our church and asked him for the name of a family that was encountering hard times. He gave me the name and address of a missionary family who had just returned from the mission field. They were going through financial difficulties because much of their support monies had not materialized.

My wife and I shared with our two daughters our plan. We decided to start helping the family during the first part of December and continue till just before Christmas. We agreed to provide food, clothing, and money.

This excited our daughters, especially when they found out that we were not going to let this family know who we were. We told them that if the family knew who we were they would feel some obligation toward us and maybe even some embarrassment. By not knowing who was giving the gifts, the missionaries could thank God and not us.

The next few weeks were wonderful as we left groceries and clothes on their front porch. We would ring their doorbell and run like crazy. We would hide behind bushes or cars and watch as they opened their door and found the items that were left. Our daughters had great fun. Just before Christmas, we dropped by a number of gifts for the children and the parents. One of the items was a glass piggy bank. We had stuffed it full of coins and paper money.

Our family received as much joy from giving as the missionary family probably did from receiving. Both of our families praised God for His great blessings.

**If the world is cold,
make it your business to build fires.**
Horace Traubel

A number of years ago I saw a movie entitled *The Family Who Changed the World*. The storyline revolved around the concept that the only world you can change is the one you live in. As you change the world you live in you begin to affect the world at large.

Edward Kimball was a man who changed his world. He never became rich or famous. He not only gave his money to help others, but he also gave his time and service and faithfully taught Sunday school in a church in Boston.

Attending Edward's Sunday school class was a 17-year-old young man who was not a believer. He had never personally received Christ as his Savior. This burdened the teacher's heart. Edward spent time with the young man and eventually led him to the Lord. Very few people remember the name of Edward Kimball, but many people remember the name of the young man—Dwight L. Moody. Moody, who later founded the Moody Bible Institute in Chicago, had a great Christian impact in the United States and internationally.

Jesus said,

> You are the salt of the earth. But if the salt loses its saltiness, how can it be made salty again? It is no longer good for anything, except to be thrown out and trampled by men. You are the light of the world. A city on a hill cannot be hidden. Neither do people light a lamp and put it under a bowl. Instead they put it on its stand, and it gives light to everyone in the house. In the same way, let your light shine before men, that they may see your good deeds and praise your Father in heaven (Matthew 5:13-16 NIV).

The saltiness Jesus was referring to is the penetrating effect that we have as we introduce people to Christ. As they come to know Him, their lives are transformed and they desire to pass on this good news. We have been encouraged by our Savior to make disciples of others. They, in turn, follow our example and soon there becomes a far-reaching ripple effect that influences far beyond our individual social circles. If you discipled one person per year for Christ for 40 years you would produce 40 disciples. On the other hand, if you discipled one other person who did the same thing, who did the same thing, and so on, it would have staggering results. In 20 years your investment would produce 1,048,576 disciples! In 30 years the number would grow to 1,073,700,000! All of this from your being faithful to disciple one person.

Being a Christian is more than making sure our salvation is sealed and we are going to heaven. It is also helping others share the same experience. It is living a Christlike life that demonstrates itself in service. James, the brother of Jesus, said, "Religion that God our Father accepts as pure and faultless is this: to look after orphans and widows in their distress and to keep oneself from being polluted by the world" (James 1:27 NIV). By being concerned for others our "good deeds" bring glory to God. By doing this, we become the "light of the world" that Jesus spoke of.

Somebody should tell us, right at the start of our lives, that we are dying. Then we might live life to the limit, every minute of every day. Do it! I say. Whatever you want to do, do it now! There are only so many tomorrows.

Michael Landon

Listed below are a few suggested areas where you could help to be the salt of the earth, where the light of Christ's love and goodness can shine through you to help change the world you live in. Remember, a candle loses nothing of its light by lighting another candle.

Adoption services	Book distribution
Assisting the elderly	Building homes
Assisting the grieving	Child abuse
Assisting widows	Church service
Big Brother programs	Citizen's patrols
Big Sister programs	Community clean-up projects

Crisis Pregnancy Centers

Daycare programs

Emergency aid

Food baskets

Foreign exchange students

Helping single parents

Home repairs

Hospice

Hotline counseling

Library work

Working with the mentally disadvantaged

Mission programs

Neighborhood Watch groups

Orphanages

Park maintenance

Working with the physically disadvantaged

Prison ministry

Reading to blind

Recycling programs

Retirement centers

Serving meals

Spousal abuse awareness groups

Teaching English as a Second Language

Teaching reading skills

Tutoring

Visiting hospitals

Visiting shut-ins

Voter registration drives

Youth programs

Several years ago there was a movement started that encouraged "Random Acts of Kindness." The concept was designed to encourage us to think of others rather than ourselves. These acts of kindness were designed to surprise the receiver and catch them off guard. They could take on almost any form, including leaving a larger than normal tip to a hardworking waitress or waiter, mowing someone's lawn, and babysitting.

I heard of one man who had been upgraded to first class on an airplane flight. As he was waiting to board the plane, he noticed a young mother with a small child. She looked very tired and worn out. He approached her and traded his first-class seat for her economy seat.

If you would like to bring joy into your life, do some random acts of kindness for others. As you do this, the burden of your own difficulties will lighten. Is it time to turn from looking at your trials and think of others? Ask God to open your eyes to the needs of others. Ask Him to give you a creative spirit to display His love through you.

One man gives freely, yet gains even more; another withholds unduly, but comes to poverty. A generous man will prosper; he who refreshes others will himself be refreshed.

Proverbs 11:24,25 NIV

Dear God,

It is so easy to get lost in the forest of life's problems. I have been so wrapped up in my own confusion, frustration, and darkness that I have forgotten about others. Help me to first see the needs of my family since it is so easy to pass over their struggles. Then, God, please open my eyes to see others and their personal battles. I want to be an encourager to those who are burdened. Help me reach out to others in the same way Christ reached out to me. Give me an expanded vision of the world around me. May I look through Your eyes with Your love and endeavor to help others. Amen.

Finding Our Purpose Gives Us Motivation

10

> *"Would you tell me, please, which way I ought to walk from here?"*
>
> *"That depends a good deal on where you want to get to," said the Cat.*
>
> *"I don't much care where"—said Alice.*
>
> *"Then it doesn't matter which way you go," said the Cat.*
>
> Lewis Carroll, *Alice's Adventures in Wonderland*

I'M SURE THAT YOU HAVE HEARD ABOUT the husband and wife who were traveling to visit friends when they realized they were lost. The wife said, "Honey, why don't you stop and ask for directions." "No," came his response. After a little while the wife said, "Honey, why don't you stop and get a road map?" "No," came his response. A few more minutes passed and the wife said, "Honey, you could call our friends, and they could tell us how to get there." "No," came his response. "Why not?" his wife finally asked. "Because it's against my nature as a man to stop and ask for directions or help."

We smile because this humor has an element of truth in it. It is difficult to ask for assistance; it is difficult to ask for directions. Sometimes we would rather face death than the dishonor of admitting we need help. The question we should be asking is, "Which takes more time: stopping to buy a map or getting lost?" A Chinese proverb says, "The journey of a thousand miles begins with one step." This is very true, but the bigger question is, "Where do you want to go on your journey?"

What would you like to spend your time on? How do you envision your future? Do you have any goals or plans? The old saying is still true: "If you aim at nothing, you'll hit it every time." It is important to have a map, to have direction, to have goals.

Lost, yesterday, somewhere between
sunrise and sunset, two golden hours,
each set with sixty diamond minutes.
No reward is offered, for they are gone forever.

Horace Mann

Without goals and a sense of direction we throw away time, energy, and money. Time slips away, and we grow older without our dreams being fulfilled. Imagine sitting in a rocking chair in a retirement center talking with others who are advanced in years. Can you hear the conversation? "I wish I would have done that when I was younger." "I wish I had taken time to enjoy such and such." "I wish I could go back and start over." When Nadine Stair was 86 years of age she wrote these words:

> If I had my life to live over again, I'd dare to make more mistakes next time. I'd relax. I'd limber up. I'd be sillier than I've been this trip. I would take fewer things seriously. I would take more chances, I would take more trips, I would climb more mountains and swim more rivers. I would eat more ice cream and less beans. I would, perhaps, have more actual troubles but fewer imaginary ones. You see, I'm one of those people who was sensible and sane, hour after hour, day after day.

> Oh, I've had my moments. If I had it to do over again, I'd have more of them. In fact, I'd try to have nothing else—just moments, one after another, instead of living so many years ahead of each day. I've been one of those persons who never goes anywhere without a thermometer, a hot-water bottle, a raincoat, and a parachute. If I could do it again, I would travel lighter than I have.

> If I had my life to live over, I would start barefoot earlier in the spring and stay that way later in the fall. I would go to more dances, I would ride more merry-go-rounds, I would pick more daisies.

Now is the time to pick daisies. Now is the time to make big goals. Now is the first day of the rest of your life.

Life Goals

How long do you think you will live? What is your life expectancy? Listed on the next page is a life expectancy chart from the IRS (date unkown). Of course, no one knows for sure how long they will live—that is in God's hands. The chart does, however, give a general timeframe that will help you plan for the future.

Life Expectancy

Current Age	Additional Years	Current Age	Additional Years	Current Age	Additional Years
10	71.7	40	42.5	70	16
11	70.5	41	41.5	71	15.3
12	69.7	42	40.6	72	14.6
13	68.8	43	39.6	73	13.9
14	67.8	44	38.7	74	13.2
15	66.8	45	37.7	75	12.5
16	65.8	46	36.8	76	11.9
17	64.8	47	35.9	77	11.2
18	63.9	48	34.9	78	10.6
19	62.9	49	33	79	10
20	61.9	50	33.1	80	9.5
21	60.9	51	32.2	81	8.9
22	59.9	52	31.3	82	8.4
23	59	53	30	83	7.9
24	58	54	29.5	84	7.4
25	57	55	28.6	85	6.9
26	56	56	27.7	86	6.5
27	55.1	57	26.8	87	6.1
28	54.1	58	25.9	88	5.7
29	53.1	59	25	89	5.3
30	52.2	60	24.2	90	5
31	51.2	61	23.3	91	4.7
32	50.2	62	22.5	92	4.4
33	49.3	63	21.6	93	4.1
34	48.3	64	20.8	94	3.9
35	47.3	65	20	95	3.7
36	46.4	66	19.2	96	3.4
37	45.4	67	18.4	97	3.2
38	44.4	68	17.6	98	3
39	43.5	69	16.8	99	2.8

Once you have discovered your approximate life expectancy on the chart, look at the next chart. It is another way to focus on the estimated time you have to do all the things you would like to accomplish. It primarily deals with the productive years ahead of you.

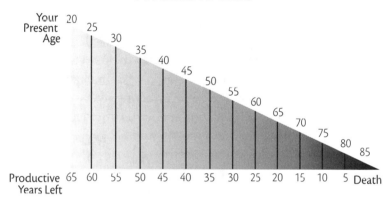

Productive Years

What are your plans for the future?

What would you like to experience? What would you like to learn or be part of in the days ahead? Is there something you would like to shape or change before you run out of time? Will there be something you leave behind that will be better than what you found?

Regardless of your age, you can do more than you think. You may have a desire to go back to school but think you are too old. You may see a need to retrain for a new vocation but think it would take too much time. You may want to move to a new area of the country but think you can't afford it. You may desire to change in a number of ways but think it will take too much energy. You may long to try something different but you are afraid. Theodore Roosevelt said, "If we are to be a really great people, we must strive in good faith to play a great part in the world. We cannot avoid meeting great issues. All that we can determine for ourselves is whether we shall meet them well or ill."

Make no little plans; they have no magic
to stir men's blood and probably themselves
will not be realized. Make big plans; aim high
in hope and work, remembering that
a noble, logical diagram once recorded
will never die, but long after we are gone
will be a living thing, asserting itself with
ever-growing insistency. Remember that your
sons and grandsons are going to do things
that would stagger us.

Daniel H. Burnham

Let's imagine you would like to go back to school to get a degree. It will take time, and you will probably have to go to night school. It may take two to four years of your life. Charles Buxton said, "You will never find time for anything. If you want time you must make it." It will take money for tuition and books. Returning to school takes a whole lot of energy—especially if you have to work during the day, go to school at night, and study on the weekends. Do you think you're too old?

I went back to school and started working toward a master's degree in counseling when I was 34. I was married with two children and working full time. Most of the classes were held at night. It was difficult, but as I look back I am very glad I took the step. After completing the master's degree program, I logged the 3,000-plus hours required for the California Marriage, Child, and Family Counseling license and took the state board examination. I actually logged 4,200 hours of counseling experience. I lost 1,200 hours because they were not under the supervision that was accepted by the State of California! (How is that for a real groaner?) At 46, I started into a Ph.D. program in counseling. School was not any easier this time, and I was still working full time. I am glad that I toughed it out—but don't ask me if I'd like to do it again!

Let me ask you a question. How old are you right now? All right, here is another question: If you don't go to school, how old will you be in four years? How old will you be in four years if you do go to school? Either way, you will be four years older. Do you want to be four years older with an education or four years older without an education? That is the real question. Time flies, but you are the navigator. Each moment you put off making decisions life is passing you by.

Great minds have purpose, others have wishes.
Washington Irving

Deciding on Goals

The next step toward taking charge of your life is writing down the goals you would like to accomplish. Until you write them down and begin to act on them, they are only dreams. It has been estimated that 95 percent of businesspeople do not have written goals. Of the 5 percent who write down their goals, they reach 95 percent of them.

The following goal sheet is broken into nine areas: spiritual goals, goals with spouse, goals with children, educational goals, vocational goals, financial goals, service goals, community goals, personal goals, and miscellaneous goals. Take some time and list what you would like to see accomplished in each category. Make the goals as specific as possible. For example; instead of writing "I will read more," make it specific: "I will read 20 books this year."

When I first started listing my goals, a frightening thing happened. In a six-month period of time, I had reached all of them. That's when I realized I needed to have more goals and aim higher. You, too, will need to revisit and renew your goals about every six months. This gives you the opportunity to cross off the goals you have reached and add new ones to the list. Keep a list of all the goals you accomplish. This will help you realize the power of goal setting and encourage you to continue setting them.

Goals

Spiritual Goals

1.

2.

3.

4.

5.

6.

7.

8.

9.

10.

Goals with Spouse

1.

2.

3.

4.

5.

6.

7.

8.

9.

10.

Goals with Children

1.

2.

3.

4.

5.

6.

7.

8.

9.

10.

Educational Goals

1.

2.

3.

4.

5.

6.

7.

8.

9.

10.

Vocational Goals

1.

2.

3.

4.

5.

6.

7.

8.

9.

10.

Financial Goals

1.

2.

3.

4.

5.

6.

7.

8.

9.

10.

Service Goals

1.

2.

3.

4.

5.

6.

7.

8.

9.

10.

Community Goals

1.

2.

3.

4.

5.

6.

7.

8.

9.

10.

Personal Goals

1.

2.

3.

4.

5.

6.

7.

8.

9.

10.

11.

12.

13.

14.

15.

16.

17.

18.

19.

20.

Miscellaneous Goals

1.

2.

3.

4.

5.

6.

7.

8.

9.

10.

11.

12.

13.

14.

15.

16.

17.

18.

19.

20.

Reinforcing Your Drive to Change

One of the things that helps in goal-setting are problems. Difficulties make us want to change; facing tough times provides strong motivation. Remember, we only change when we hurt enough. Discomfort can be a driving force for making adjustment. Don't resent trouble. Welcome it as a friend. Learn to cooperate with the inevitable.

> Have mercy on me, O God, have mercy on me, for in you my soul takes refuge. I will take refuge in the shadow of your wings until the disaster has passed. I cry out to God Most High, to God, who fulfills [his purpose] for me. He sends from heaven and saves me…(Psalm 57:1-3 NIV, brackets in original).

As you look at your goal list, thank God for the troubles that give you motivation and determination to change. Commitment is the ability to bind oneself emotionally and intellectually to an idea or task that needs to be completed. A classic example of commitment to a goal was the Spanish conquistador Hernando Cortéz. On an expedition to Mexico, he was in charge of 500 men on 11 ships. After leaving Cuba, they landed on the coast of the Yucatan in the year 1519. To ensure that his men were committed to their task—to their goal—Cortéz burned all of the ships except one so no one could back out. They were forced to move forward.

God will give you the courage to burn your ships of hurt, pain, loss, anger, fear, unforgiveness, depression, worry, low self-image, procrastination, and old habits if you ask Him. It's difficult, but vital to forget the past and let it burn away. Move forward with determination to create your new future. Don't turn back.

In the process of discovering your purpose and carrying out your goals, surround yourself with positive people. Their energy and enthusiasm will encourage you and help you find the strength to face the tough times:

> Blessed is the man who does not walk in the counsel of the wicked or stand in the way of sinners or sit in the seat of mockers. But his delight is in the law of the LORD, and on his law he meditates day and night. He is like a tree planted by streams of water, which yields its fruit in season and whose leaf does not wither. Whatever he does prospers (Psalm 1:1-3 NIV).

Have you ever watched wind surfers in the ocean or on a lake? The board they ride looks like a surfboard with a sail. The riders make sharp turns and change direction quickly—and make it look effortless. Some decisions in life are as smooth as how wind surfers handle their crafts. They can be made quickly and effortlessly. Deciding what flavor of ice cream you like to eat is not a major decision. To decide to stop when the traffic light turns red is a "no brainer." Receiving a Christmas gift doesn't require a committee meeting. But the harder, larger decisions in life are like ocean liners. They do not change direction quickly. It takes a lot of room and several miles for a large ship to change course. People who watch a large ship turn around think, *This sure takes a long time.* The same will be true for some of the decisions you will face. Don't be discouraged if you don't see immediate results.

Until one is committed, there is hesitancy, the chance to draw back, always ineffectiveness. There is one elementary truth, the ignorance of which kills countless ideas and splendid plans, that the moment one definitely commits oneself then providence moves too. All sorts of things begin to occur which would never otherwise have occurred, and a whole stream of events issues from the decision, raising in one's favor all manner of unforeseen incidents and material assistance which no man could have dreamt would have come his way. I have learned a deep respect for one of Goethe's couplets: Boldness has genius, power, and magic in it.

W.H. Murray

Have you ever tried to turn the steering wheel of a large truck that is fully loaded and the engine is off? It is almost impossible. You have to first start the engine, shift the truck into gear, and start rolling *before* you can really turn the steering wheel. Making a decision to change is like starting the engine. Shifting into gear is like writing down your goals. The truck starting to roll is your commitment to action. Do not expect any changes in your life until these events have taken place. And remember, large trucks or large ships are not like wind surfers—they can't make quick changes in direction just because they are moving. It takes time. But, eventually, even a small turn in the wheel will change the direction of the largest of vehicles.

Three Rules of Work
1. Out of clutter, find simplicity.
2. From discord, find harmony.
3. In the middle of difficulty, find opportunity.

Albert Einstein

Getting Organized

How would you like three extra months a year? Would this help you get everything done? It is estimated that we spend up to six weeks a year looking for stuff. Imagine that—a month and a half! We could gain over a month's period of time just by getting organized. This is what Einstein meant when he said, "Out of clutter, find simplicity." Not only does clutter hide things, it sucks creativity and energy from your brain. What are the ramifications of getting organized? It means some things have to be thrown away. This will be hard for some individuals. Getting organized means turning off the television, not going golfing, and not shopping. It means cleaning out the garage, organizing a closet, and straightening the drawer by the telephone. And it means throwing away magazines, junk mail, outdated and underused possessions. The process of throwing things away can be softened by having a garage sale so you can earn a little money for your effort. Or you could give items to the Salvation Army or your favorite charity.

Organizing starts by creating files for things you would like to keep. This includes important information that needs to be read or kept for future retrieval. This important information does not include hate mail that you have received over the years. Burn those items just as Cortéz burned the ships. No turning back. You don't need those reminders.

You will also have to learn to say *no*. This means you might need to resign from some committees or boards. It means some people may be upset with you because you are not doing what they would like you to do. You might even have to regain control if your schedule is too busy and too stressful.

Several years ago I attended a conference for counselors. I met another counselor, and we shared what we did in our counseling practices. After a period of time the man looked at me and said, "I think you are a pretty good counselor. How long are you going to last?" His words haunted me. He had a good point because I was burning the candle at both ends. I realized that it was survival time for me, and I wanted to be a counselor for the long haul. I went home and reorganized my life. I cut my schedule back and began to say no.

Getting organized gives you freedom and control. It helps you avoid conflicts and guilt and the need to perform. It might even give you extra time to relax.

I haven't forgotten about the other 2 months I mentioned earlier. You can gain them by getting up one hour earlier each day. This will give you 365 extra hours. Divide that by 8 working hours a day times 5 days, times 4 weeks a month, and you come up with more than 2 extra months a year to accomplish some of the things you would like to do. This will give you time to exercise each day or meditate more or increase your reading time. It will give you time to study if you are going back to school or want to update your skills. You may even wish to spend some time exploring your spiritual gifts (see Romans 12, 1 Corinthians 12–14, and Ephesians 4).

Listed below are some of the gifts that may be part of God's plan and purpose for you. Taken from Patrick M. Morley's book *The Rest of Your Life*, this list was adapted from the work of Carl Smith, Kenneth O. Gangel, and Leslie B. Flynn.

> *Mercy:* Special ability to show sympathy to the suffering saints—meals to the sick, hospital visits, phone calls, and visits to the hurting.

> *Service:* Special ability to joyfully serve behind the scenes—set up chairs, usher, assist leaders.

> *Hospitality:* Special desire to offer a place to meet, food, and lodging—host missionaries, Bible studies, reach out to others.

> *Giving:* Special desire and financial ability to give—generosity toward youth mission trips, offerings, parachurch ministries, the needs of the pastor.

> *Administration:* Special ability to orchestrate program details—committee work, church office needs, conference/seminar supervision.

> *Leadership:* Special ability to preside or govern wisely—boards of Christian ministries, elders, deacons, committee chairperson, nursery programs, fundraising.

> *Faith:* Vision for new projects and the perseverance to see them through—building programs, new ministries.

Discernment: Ability to detect error—meet with teachers to discuss curriculi, letters to the editor, evaluate programs and teaching.

It must be borne in mind that the tragedy of life doesn't lie in not reaching your goal. The tragedy lies in having no goal to reach. It isn't a calamity to die with dreams unfilled, but it is a calamity not to dream. It is not a disgrace not to reach the stars, but it is a disgrace to have no stars to reach for. Not failure, but low aim, is a sin.

Helmut Schmidt

Dear God,

Please help me take a hard look at my life and what I have been doing. I need to develop some goals—not just little ones, but long-term ones. Help me stretch in this area. Please give me some new thoughts about what You think I should be doing.

Help me stop procrastinating and get organized and throw away all the clutter in my life. I have wasted much valuable time that is lost forever. Help me schedule myself better.

Father, please help me discover my spiritual gifts and learn to use them for Your service. I want to stop looking at myself; I want to start helping others. I know my life has to change. Please start by helping me turn my steering wheel, start the engine, and move forward. Amen.

Designing and Implementing Your 42-Day Plan

11

More powerful than the will to win, is the courage to begin. He who steps out the door already has a good part of his journey behind him.

Author unknown

WHEN JUDY FIRST CAME FOR COUNSELING she was severely depressed. She didn't have any motivation to do normal housework or even go shopping with friends. She broke into tears easily and sometimes spoke in angry tones.

Judy and her mother had not spoken to each other for the last three months. They had been in an off-and-on battle since she was a teenager. After she married Rick and had their first child, the tension between Judy and her mom progressed. Her mother continually told her how to take care of the baby and how to clean house. Judy was sick and tired of the whole mess.

Rick, too, was tired of all the raw emotions. He had listened to Judy's complaints until he could stand it no longer.

He began to tell Judy to grow up and get over it. This did not help their marital adjustment.

Judy had come to the place where the pain was so great that she did not know what to do. She was angry with her mother, angry with Rick, angry with God, and angry with herself. She had finally come a point where she was hurting so much that she knew she had to change or she might do something drastic. She had been contemplating escaping from all the pain through suicide.

After several sessions she realized she needed to make peace with her pain and peace with others. Her anger was destroying her, and she knew it. The hardest hurdle for her to jump over was forgiving her mother. This was not an easy task and took several weeks before she could muster up the courage to do it.

We talked about what she would like to achieve and how to get there. We talked about motivation and how to begin making positive steps forward. I shared that there are two ways to get started. One was to begin dealing with small issues in her life, such as cleaning her house, ironing, and helping neighbors. Having victory in small areas would give her motivation to overcome larger areas of difficulty.

The other method for getting started was to deal with the large issues first and then go to the smaller issues. This would entail going to her mother, admitting her anger, and asking for forgiveness. This would be hard, but after that everything else would be easier to conquer. She would be on a downhill run, increasing the speed of change. Either method will work because both are like the question: "How do you eat an elephant?" The answer is, "One bite at a time." Change does not happen all at once. Life is a continuing process of growth through struggles.

Judy had to think about the concepts of small to big, or big to small for a period of time. She chose to take the faster route. She went for the big first and went directly to her mother. There was a real sense of freedom and release when Judy finally forgave her mother. Her next battle was to forgive herself for her anger at God and at Rick. When this was accomplished, a great fear overcame her. She was afraid she would fall back into the same old patterns of anger and resentment. She knew she had to set up a plan to change her old habits and style of behavior.

**Nothing is particularly hard
if you divide it into small jobs.**
Henry Ford

Making changes start in the test tube of trouble and trials. As we contemplate the pain of what we are facing, our motivation is ignited. As motivation builds, we begin to figure out how to deal with our difficult issues. This leads us to action through courage and faith. Freedom and victory come as we conquer our fears and apprehensions. Peace is developed as we begin to maintain a new pattern of living. This excitement encourages us to share our journey with others. And then the spiral of change can begin in their lives.

You Can Do It!

It sometimes takes time for our emotions to catch up with our intellect and our actions. We must learn to act regardless of how we are feeling. Our actions will lead our feelings to a change point. If we wait until we feel like acting, we may never do anything!

For example, if you are in a relationship struggle with other people and your feelings have been hurt, it slows down your positive actions toward them. After you've been hurt, you forgive them and ask for forgiveness yourself. You even begin to act in a positive manner toward them...but your emotions will still be a little raw from the experience. The *frequency* of conflict will diminish before the *intensity* of the conflict decreases. William James said, "It is easier to act yourself into feeling, than to feel yourself into acting."

Even cowards can endure hardships;
only the brave can endure suspense.

Mignon McLaughlin

Are there issues you are facing that need to be changed? Are there relationships that need to be reconciled and restored? Do any of the following items register as areas you need to work on? Are there other areas that are not mentioned that you are struggling with?

Problem Areas

Alcohol	Hair pulling
Anorexia	Hatefulness
Argumentative attitude	Jaw clenching
Bitterness	Jealousy
Boredom	Knee jiggling
Broken relationships	Lack of commitment
Bulemia	Laziness
Caffeine addiction	Lip biting
Chewing fingernails	Living in past
Cracking knuckles	Lying
Cracking neck	Not keeping secrets
Critical spirit	Obsessiveness
Disloyalty	Pessimistic and negative
Doubts	Procrastination
Drugs	Promise breaking
Envy	Rapid eating
Extramarital affair	Rebellion
Fantasies	Regret
Fears	Resentment
Fidgeting	Sexual problems
Finger-tapping	Sloppiness
Forgetfulness	Smoking
Gambling	Snacking
Gluttony	Stealing
Gossip	Tics
Guilt	Toe tapping
Gum snapping	Worry

One of the big factors in changing lifestyles and relationships is procrastination. The word comes from the Latin *pro,* which means forward motion, and *crastinus,* which means belonging to tomorrow. Procrastination is putting off something burdensome or unpleasant. It is not doing something you know you really should do. It is the belief that taking action would be more painful than putting it off.

We all tend to avoid pain. We all want guarantees that everything will be all right. We tell ourselves that we will wait for the "magical moment"—when the time is just right. We engage in wishful thinking. Some of us even deserve a gold medal for how well we procrastinate. Gloria Pitzer said it this way,

> Procrastination is my sin.
> It brings me naught but sorrow.
> I know that I should stop it.
> In fact, I will—tomorrow!

Sometimes we tell ourselves: "If I only had more time." "If I only had more money." "If I had a more secure job." "I'll wait until I feel better." "I'll do it tomorrow." Little do we realize that when we postpone any action, things get worse. We get older. We put on more weight. We become unhealthy and out of shape. As we spin our wheels, we dig deeper holes in our emotions and deeper ruts in our habits. We tell ourselves, "I can always quit." "I have the strength to do this; I just don't want to."

Why do we procrastinate? It might be that we are simply lazy. We don't like to put out effort or emotions that are difficult or time consuming. Sometimes our anger turns inward, and we punish ourselves. At other times, we procrastinate to get even or punish others. Procrastination can occur when we are overwhelmed and under a great deal of stress. It can be filled with fear of failure, fear of rejection, or fear of criticism. Procrastination continues because there is a reward of some kind. What do you get from putting things off?

_____

Putting off an easy thing makes it hard, and putting off a hard one makes it impossible.

George Horace Lorimer

_____

It's time to throw off procrastination and get started! Today. Right now. The next chart will help you crystallize areas of change you would like to make. Take a few moments to review it, and ask God to help you map out a plan of attack to change your future in a positive way.

Desired Changes

1. *Who:* I am struggling with the following person(s) at this time in my life:

2. *What:* I am presently struggling with the following issue(s) or bad habits:

3. **_Where:_** The location where most of these struggles take place is:

4. **_When:_** These struggles usually appear (time/days/ holidays/etc.):

5. **_Why:_** I have allowed these struggles to overwhelm me because:

6. **_How:_** The things that contribute to or set up my struggles are:

7. I would like to see the following changes take place:

8. I need to forgive the following people:

9. I need to confront the following people or behaviors:

10. The first thing I plan to do is:

11. The second thing I plan to do is:

12. My commitment to begin this change is (date/place):

The mind unlearns with difficulty
what has long been impressed on it.
A nail is driven out by another nail;
habit is overcome by habit.

It takes approximately 42 days to firmly establish patterns of behavior. For example, let's take smoking. When a person smokes their first cigarette, it is not a pleasant experience. With the first attempt at inhaling the individual coughs, chokes, and his or her body rebels at having smoke in the lungs.

It is only by repeated attempts that people learn how to bring smoke into their bodies without coughing. Why would someone keep up this type of behavior? Because there is a reward. It may be in the effects received from the nicotine. Smoking could help the individual feel accepted by a group. The person might believe smoking is "cool." Regardless of the motivation, in six weeks of smoking, an individual can be locked into a smoking habit that may control him or her for a long time.

I come from a family of smokers. My grandfather smoked a pipe, and my father smoked cigarettes. Many of their friends and many of my other relatives smoked. I can remember as a child being accidentally burned by these people at various times. Later in life, my father developed lung problems that eventually led to his death. I attempted to smoke on several occasions. I thought it was the "in" thing to do. However, I could not get past the faulty logic of putting smoke into my lungs. I didn't like smoke in my lungs or eyes around a campfire, so why would I deliberately do that with a cigarette? I stopped the behavior before it became a habit.

How do we break habit patterns? By establishing new behaviors and ending old behaviors. How long does it take? Six weeks—42 days. With many habits, these six weeks of change are difficult. A swearing habit does not end overnight. Giving up drugs or alcohol are not pleasant experiences since they create a dependency in the body.

It's important to be wise in the process of change. I remember counseling one man who drank 15 cups of coffee a day. When he was not drinking coffee, he was drinking soft drinks filled with caffeine. He was nervous, having trouble sleeping at night, and had stomach and bowel problems. I suggested he consider getting off caffeine, but forgot to tell him to not do it all at once. Being a tough man (he thought), he stopped overnight. As a result, he became sick and could not go to work for three days due to the withdrawal symptoms.

Once we determine to change our behavior, we will find it a difficult task to complete. The first three weeks are very critical. There will be strong desires to stay with the old way because change doesn't happen quickly. Don't give up at this point. Continue for the full 42 days!

42-Day Guarantee

Sometimes in my counseling practice, when counseling married couples, I suggest a 42-day plan. I tell them, "If you do what I suggest for six weeks, you will feel differently and your marriage will become healthy. If you follow my recommendations and you don't feel better, I will refund your money." No one has ever come back for a refund.

On pages 173-76, you considered areas of your life you would like to change or modify. If you are feeling down or discouraged, there is hope for you. You can feel great in 42 days! Is this really possible? Yes! Why not give it a try?

I wish I could be present to personally help you through this process. The next best thing is to encourage you with meditating thoughts for the 42 days to change. The next section includes a 42-day devotional and some powerful Scriptures that will give you courage. Every day read several of these Scriptures that are applicable to your exciting journey of change. To further inspire you, I've included a 12-step program written by Reverend Vernon Bittner at the Minnesota-based Institute for Christian Living. It is a helpful reminder of your commitment to change.

Dear God,

I have been feeling a lot of pain and discouragement for a long time. I have been overpowered by critical and negative thoughts. My pessimistic thinking has worn a deep rut in my mind. I don't think I can climb out of the rut by myself. Please help me. I want to see new vistas instead of the bottom of this ditch I am in. I want to take the plunge into a new way of thinking and living.

Please wash my mind with new thoughts. I want to change how I have been viewing my problems. I am going to need Your help and strength. Please encourage me with the commitment and determination to continue for the next 42 days.

I can hardly wait to see what You are going to do! Amen.

Daily Thoughts for Your Journey

12 Steps for Christian Living

Help from the Bible

Jesus Will Help You!

Daily Thoughts for
Your Journey

The only measure of what you believe is what you do. If you want to know what people believe, don't read what they write, don't ask them what they believe, just observe what they do.

Ashley Montagu

As YOU BEGIN YOUR 42-DAY JOURNEY to feeling great, ask God to give you a spirit of enthusiasm and excitement. Regardless of the circumstances you face, there is a light at the end of the tunnel. And that light comes from Jesus Christ.

For the next 42 days I encourage you to read the corresponding devotions. They begin with a topic to focus on followed by: a Scripture verse to review and ponder, a thought to encourage you, a quote to inspire you, and additional Scriptures to help you draw on God's strength and wisdom. I suggest you spend a few minutes at the beginning of each day to read the devotional and look up the "encouragers." At the end of your meditation time, ask God to help you with any struggles you may face with regard to the topic for the day. These readings will comfort you and help you as you go through the stages of change. If you follow the devotional plan for 42 days, you will be amazed by the changes in your life!

Day 1

Affliction

We can rejoice, too, when we run into problems and trials, for we know that they are good for us—they help us learn to endure (Romans 5:3).

It is not fun to encounter hardships, sufferings, and trials. As a matter of fact, it is often very painful. In the midst of problems, it is easy to become lost in all of the hurt. If you focus on the discomfort, your motivation for change will decrease. As you begin your 42-day journey, ask God to help you learn from your circumstances. Ask Him to give you the strength to endure with patience your present trials and experience the joy of growing spiritually.

Affliction comes to us all not to make us sad, but sober; not to make us sorry, but wise; not to make us despondent, but by its darkness to refresh us, as the night refreshes the day; not to impoverish, but to enrich us, as the plow enriches the field; to multiply our joy, as the seed, by planting, is multiplied a thousandfold.

Henry Ward Beecher

Encouragers

Psalm 119:67,68,71
Romans 5:3-5
James 1:2,3

Day 2

Anger

A fool gives full vent to anger, but a wise person quietly holds it back (Proverbs 29:11).

Anger is a signal that something is wrong. Who or what is the focus of your ire? Is your feeling based on a real or an "imagined" hurt? If your anger is imagined, ask God to help you view the situation correctly. If it is real, confess it to the one who hurt you and ask God for the grace to forgive him or her. Speak the truth in love, and attempt to reconcile the relationship. Don't let anger grow and fester in your soul.

Frequent fits of anger produce in the soul a propensity to be angry; which ofttimes ends in a choler, bitterness, and morosity, when the mind becomes ulcerated, peevish, and querulous, and is wounded by the least occurrence.

Plutarch

Encouragers

Proverbs 15:1,4,18
Proverbs 19:11
Ephesians 4:26-32

Day 3

Fear

I prayed to the LORD, and he answered me, freeing me from all my fears (Psalm 34:4).

You may fear the loss of a job, a material possession, a relationship, or respect. Your fear might be related to facing danger or losing security. What loss are you facing? Is it real or imagined? You can deal with fear by acknowledging to God what you are feeling. Fear is your friend when it drives you into the arms of God. Let Him know, through prayer, that you need His comfort and strength. Trust Him to lead and be with you.

Many of our fears are tissue paper-thin, and a single courageous step would carry us clear through them.

Brendan Francis

Encouragers

Psalm 27:1
Isaiah 41:10,13
Romans 8:35-39

Day 4

Hatred

Get rid of all bitterness, rage, anger, harsh words, and slander, as well as all types of malicious behavior. Instead, be kind to each other, tenderhearted, forgiving one another, just as God through Christ has forgiven you (Ephesians 4:31,32).

Hate is a very powerful emotion. It has the strength to divide families, end relationships, and cause damage to physical health. Hate destroys happiness and mental well-being.

The emotion of hate is tied to your thinking process. If you want to get rid of hate, you must begin thinking about the positives of the situation rather than the negatives. Hate does not help your circumstances; it adds to your misery. Ask God to help you get this monster off your back.

Hating people is like burning down your own house to get rid of a rat.

H.E. Fosdick

Encouragers

Leviticus 19:17
Romans 12:14-19
Hebrews 12:14,15

Day 5

Worry

So don't worry about tomorrow, for tomorrow will bring its own worries. Today's trouble is enough for today (Matthew 6:34).

Someone said, "It pays to worry because 90 percent of the things I worry about never happen. Worry keeps them away." Worry consumes your thoughts and makes you unproductive—and it changes absolutely nothing! The opposite of worry is trust. If you are worrying, then you are not trusting God. Do you think God is caught off guard by your problems? If He cares about the birds of the air—and the Bible says He does—He cares about what you are facing. Drop your worries at His doorstep.

Worry is a thin stream of fear trickling through the mind. If encouraged, it cuts a channel into which all other thoughts are drained.

A.S. Roche

Encouragers

Psalm 23
Psalm 55:22
Matthew 6:25-34

Day 6

Revenge

Dear friends, never avenge yourselves. Leave that to God. For it is written, "I will take vengeance; I will repay those who deserve it," says the Lord (Romans 12:19).

Almost everyone who has been hurt has thought, "This is not fair; this is not right." Thoughts of unfairness give rise to the desire to get even or seek retribution. Revenge drops you to the same level (or below) as the person who has done you wrong. The way to peace in these situations is to give the problem to the Lord. Ask Him to help you realize that justice may not come in the form you would like to see. Remember, God will settle all accounts one day.

A man that studieth revenge keeps his own wounds green, which otherwise would heal and do well.

Francis Bacon

Encouragers

Proverbs 20:22
Proverbs 24:29
Romans 12:17-21

Day 7

Loneliness

For God has said, "I will never fail you. I will never forsake you" (Hebrews 13:5).

"For He [God] Himself has said, I will not in any way fail you nor give you up nor leave you without support. [I will] not, [I will] not, [I will] not in any degree leave you helpless nor forsake nor let [you] down (relax My hold on you)! [Assuredly not!]" (Hebrews 13:5 AMP, brackets and parentheses in original).

Solitude is the joy of being alone. Loneliness is the pain of being alone. Everyone needs someone to talk to—to share his or her life with.

When you see a beautiful sunset you can enjoy it, but it is more fulfilling to share it with someone. Are you feeling alone? "I went outside to find a friend but could not find one there; I went outside to be a friend, and friends were everywhere." Maybe it's time for you to go outside and be a friend, then you will discover that your loneliness will disappear.

The best remedy for those who are afraid, lonely, or unhappy is to go outside, somewhere where they can be quite alone with the heavens, nature, and God. Because only then does one feel that all is as it should be and that God wishes to see people happy amidst the simple beauty of nature.

Anne Frank

Encouragers

Psalm 121
Isaiah 41:10
Hebrews 13:2-6

Day 8

Suffering

So be truly glad! There is wonderful joy ahead, even though it is necessary for you to endure many trials for a while. These trials are only to test your faith, to show that it is strong and pure. It is being tested as fire tests and purifies gold—and your faith is far more precious to God than mere gold (1 Peter 1:6,7).

Suffering is not something we can avoid. All men and women face it to one degree or another. How people face this pain helps develop their characters. It is not men and women who live a life of ease that we admire; we look up to those who have overcome great adversity and have had victory over difficult circumstances. God will use the suffering you are facing to encourage others who may be going through the same situation. Don't give up before you learn the lessons that He wants you to pass on to others.

The truth that many people never understand, until it is too late, is that the more you try to avoid suffering the more you suffer because smaller and more insignificant things begin to torture you in proportion to your fear of being hurt.

Thomas Merton

Encouragers

Isaiah 43:2
Hebrews 4:14-16
1 Peter 4:12,13

Day 9

Depression

When you go through deep waters and great trouble, I will be with you. When you go through rivers of difficulty, you will not drown! When you walk through the fire of oppression, you will not be burned up; the flames will not consume you. For I am the LORD, your God, the Holy One of Israel, your Savior (Isaiah 43:2,3).

Depression makes you want to withdraw from other people and life in general. This emotion usually comes as a result of being deeply hurt by someone or encountering a specific, difficult situation. Loss, loneliness, and guilt are often found in depression, and anger is a strong component. To overcome this emotion, acknowledge the hurt, work through the anger, focus on God's great works in your past, think about what is true and right (see Philippians 4:8), and look ahead to serving the Lord.

One of the bad things about depression is that it drains us emotionally and makes us unable to handle things that normally would not get us down.

Billy Graham

Encouragers

Psalm 55
Isaiah 41:10
Philippians 4:13

Guilt

So now there is no condemnation for those who belong to Christ Jesus. For the power of the life-giving Spirit has freed you through Christ Jesus from the power of sin that leads to death (Romans 8:1,2).

Guilt, remorse, and regret for some past event may still affect your daily living. Although the past can teach lessons about God, about life, and about yourself, don't let it haunt you. Heed those lessons and move forward. You can do absolutely nothing to change the past, and trying to do so is a waste of time. Instead, focus all your energy on what you *can* do to determine the outcome of this moment, this hour, this day.

From the body of one guilty deed a thousand ghostly fears and haunting thoughts proceed.

William Wadsworth

Encouragers

Psalm 51:1-11
Romans 7:18-25
Hebrews 10:21,22

Day 11

Conscience

Cling tightly to your faith in Christ, and always keep your conscience clear. For some people have deliberately violated their consciences; as a result, their faith has been shipwrecked (1 Timothy 1:19).

During this journey to feeling great, it is important to become sensitive to the still, small voice of your conscience. Your conscience may suggest it is better to leave some things unsaid. It may tell you that you have hurt someone's feelings. This inner voice has been given to you by God to help direct your moral behavior. Your conscience helps you determine right from wrong. It tells you to forgive others and to ask for forgiveness yourself. Listen carefully and obey.

Preserve your conscience always soft and sensitive. If but one sin forces its way into that tender part of the soul and is suffered to dwell there, the road is paved for a thousand iniquities.

Isaac Watts

Encouragers

Hebrews 9:14
Hebrews 13:18
1 John 3:19,20

Day 12

Backsliding

My dear brothers and sisters, if anyone among you wanders away from the truth and is brought back again, you can be sure that the one who brings that person back will save that sinner from death and bring about the forgiveness of many sins (James 5:19,20).

"Backsliding" means going the exact opposite direction from where you want to go. Sometimes the best intentions go awry. Have you been deviating from the path you know you should be traveling? Have you been avoiding what you should be doing? Today is the day to resist the slippery slope and fight to regain solid ground. Ask God to give you firm footing and the spirit of resistance.

Sin is always the cause of a backslidden condition. We may have received Christ but now allow lying, temper, meanness, laziness, or some other bad habit, such as wrong thinking or sinful behavior, to separate us from God's blessing. Backsliding starts in the heart and then finds expression through outward action.

Billy Graham

Encouragers

1 Timothy 1:19
Hebrews 3:12,15
2 Peter 1:9

Day 13

Pride

The LORD despises pride; be assured that the proud will be punished (Proverbs 16:5).

Pride is a thinking process clouded by self-centeredness. Pride in self-sufficiency undermines faith by telling us that we do not need God and can live apart from Him. Pride blocks the ability to truly evaluate our lives and how arrogant we have become. It makes us judgmental and legalistic in our relationships with others. In some cases, loneliness is the price of pride, because people usually do not like to be around "me focused" people.

Pride is the only disease known to man that makes everyone sick except the one who has it.

Buddy Robinson

Encouragers

Proverbs 6:16,17
Proverbs 16:5,18,19
Proverbs 29:23

Day 14

Courage

I have told you all this so that you may have peace in me. Here on earth you will have many trials and sorrows. But take heart, because I have overcome the world (John 16:33).

For courage to exist, there must be at least two conditions present. The first is danger, or fear, and the second is a cause worth fighting for. Have you experienced fearful thoughts on your journey to happiness? Courage is not necessary when everything is going your way. Courage comes when you are facing difficulty and uncertainty. As for a cause worth fighting for—aren't changing your emotions and altering your lifestyle for the better fantastic reasons for exercising courage?

Last, but by no means least, courage—moral courage, the courage of one's convictions, the courage to see things through. The world is in a constant conspiracy against the brave. It's the age-old struggle—the roar of the crowd on one side and the voice of your conscience on the other.

Gen. Douglas MacArthur

Encouragers

Proverbs 28:1
2 Corinthians 12:9,10
2 Timothy 1:7

Day 15

Selfishness

What is causing the quarrels and fights among you? Isn't it the whole army of evil desires at war within you? You want what you don't have, so you scheme and kill to get it. You are jealous for what others have, and you can't possess it, so you fight and quarrel to take it away from them (James 4:1,2).

Selfishness basically separates you from God, family, and friends. "What's in it for me" thinking destroys relationships. With selfishness, privileges soon become rights and rights become demands, which lead to awkward situations and hurt feelings. Have you been acting in a selfish, demanding way? Have you been thinking about your rights so much that you have missed the needs of others? Change your focus today.

If you wish to be miserable, think about yourself—about what you want, what you like, what respect people ought to pay you, what people think of you; and then to you nothing will be pure. You will spoil everything you touch; you will make sin and misery for yourself out of everything God sends you; you will be as wretched as you choose.

Charles Kingsley

Encouragers

Romans 15:1-3
Philippians 2:4,20,21
1 John 3:17

Day 16

Laziness

But you, lazybones, how long will you sleep? When will you wake up? I want you to learn this lesson: A little extra sleep, a little more slumber, a little folding of the hands to rest—and poverty will pounce on you like a bandit; scarcity will attack you like an armed robber (Proverbs 6:9-11).

Laziness often enters our lives when we face an unpleasant task. We think that by putting off an action maybe it will disappear. When we get behind in tasks and responsibilities, our failure to perform grows until any task seems too large and requires too much energy. The value placed on the task or responsibility determines the amount of effort we will put forth to accomplish the end result. How much is it worth to you to change how you have been living and feeling?

Laziness is a secret ingredient that goes into failure. But it's only kept a secret from the person who fails.

Robert Half

Encouragers

Proverbs 6:6-11
Proverbs 10:4,5,26
Proverbs 13:4

Day 17

Temptation

Temptation comes from the lure of our own evil desires. These evil desires lead to evil actions, and evil actions lead to death (James 1:14,15).

The great Christian reformer Martin Luther said, "You can't stop the birds from flying over your head, but you can stop them from building a nest in your hair." Temptation is not the issue as much as what your response to it is. There is no temptation without previous preparation. Have you been placing yourself in temptation's playground or have you been avoiding it by traveling down a different, more godly path of thinking or exposure? Running away from temptation is a smart thing to do!

---

*No one knows how bad he is until he has tried to be good.
There is a silly idea about that good people
don't know what temptation means.*

C.S. Lewis

Encouragers

Proverbs 4:14,15
1 Corinthians 10:13,28-32
James 1:2-4,12-16

Day 18

Habits

Do not let sin control the way you live; do not give in to its lustful desires. Do not let any part of your body become a tool of wickedness, to be used for sinning (Romans 6:12,13).

People are creatures of habit. Some of our habits are good, such as brushing our teeth, and some habits are bad, such as losing our temper. Habits are developed by repeating specific actions over and over. And, usually, the only way to get rid of bad habits is to replace them with good habits. If the void of the bad habit is not filled with something good, the bad will often return.

Pick out a habit you would like to replace and a behavior to replace it with. Remember, the old habit will fight to remain, so hang in there for the full 42 days.

Habit, if not resisted, soon becomes necessity.

Saint Augustine

Encouragers

Psalm 119:9,11
Romans 6:11-14
Galatians 5:24

Day 19

Commitment

I have fought a good fight, I have finished the race, and I have remained faithful (2 Timothy 4:7).

This is a good day to examine your commitments. What are you willing to die for? What are you willing to put time, money, and energy into? What activities are you willing to back with action and not just talk? Commitment demands persistence and perseverance—a willingness to pay the cost. You are getting close to the halfway mark of 21 days. There may be many pressures to discontinue the course you are on. Ignore them. Stay committed to your 42-day plan.

To commit everything to the Lord means entrusting our life, family, job, and possessions to his control and guidance. To commit ourselves to the Lord means to trust him, believing that he can care for us better than we can ourselves.

Life Application Bible

Encouragers

Matthew 24:13
1 Corinthians 16:13,14
Galatians 6:9

Day 20

Forgiveness

You must make allowance for each other's faults and forgive the person who offends you. Remember, the Lord forgave you, so you must forgive others (Colossians 3:13).

It's hard to forgive when you're the one who is hurt. Usually we want the person who is at fault to apologize, but God asks us to forgive no matter what the situation is. Forgiveness is not based on a feeling. It is a promise—a commitment to: 1) not hold a grudge against the offender; 2) not talk to others about the offense; and 3) not dwell on the offense. In forgiveness, you give up your right to retaliate. *Forgiveness is only for the brave and courageous!*

If men wound you with injuries, meet them with patience:
hasty words rankle the wound, soft language dresses it,
forgiveness cures it, and oblivion takes away the scar.
It is more noble by silence to avoid an injury
than by argument to overcome it.

Francis Beaumont

Encouragers

Psalm 103:12
Colossians 3:12-15
1 John 1:9

Day 21

Obedience

Obedience is far better than sacrifice. Listening to him is much better than offering the fat of rams. Rebellion is as bad as the sin of witchcraft, and stubbornness is as bad as worshiping idols (1 Samuel 15:22,23).

You are at the halfway point! Your emotions may be crying out, "I still don't feel great yet." Ignore them. Keep your determination going. God does not call us to obey Him just when we feel like it. We are to trust and obey Him *regardless* of our feelings or circumstances. Do you remember the words of Job when his life was turned upside down and he was not feeling very good? "Though he slay me, yet will I hope in him" (13:15 NIV).

All who know well how to obey will know also how to rule.

Flavius Josephus

Encouragers

1 Samuel 15:22,23
Psalm 143:10
Proverbs 19:16

Day 22

Responsibility

God has given each of us the ability to do certain things well....Never be lazy in your work, but serve the Lord enthusiastically (Romans 12:6,11).

Sometimes it is not any fun to grow up. As we mature, we have to accept more and more responsibility—especially for our actions. It is far easier to blame others for our problems. As long as we can generate excuses for our behavior we do not have to change. Have you been acting responsibly or irresponsibly in the circumstances you are encountering? Is it time for you to take positive action and not wait for others to lead? Ask God to help you become the person He wants you to be.

No man will succeed unless he is ready to face and overcome difficulties—and is prepared to assume responsibilities.

William J.H. Boetoker

Encouragers

Ecclesiastes 11:9,10
Ecclesiastes 12:13,14
Romans 12:3-8

Day 23

Honesty

But most of all, my brothers and sisters, never take an oath, by heaven or earth or anything else. Just say a simple yes or no, so that you will not sin and be condemned for it (James 5:12).

Have you been dealing with your family and friends in an honest, trustworthy manner? You see, it is possible to be honest and cruel at the same time. The Bible instructs us to speak the truth in love (see Ephesians 4:15 NIV). It might be the truth to say to a family member, "You sure have a big pimple on your nose." But is it the most loving thing to say? How we communicate is just as important as what we say. How have you been doing in your relationships? Today would be a good day to speak the truth in a loving manner.

No matter how brilliant a man may be, he will never engender confidence in his subordinates and associates if he lacks simple honesty and moral courage.

J. Lawton Collins

Encouragers

Psalm 24:3-6
Proverbs 12:22
Philippians 4:8

Day 24

Confidence

Trust in the LORD and do good. Then you will live safely in the land and prosper....Commit everything you do to the LORD. Trust him, and he will help you (Psalm 37:3,5).

Confidence arises out of understanding. To have conviction, a person must study the facts and get all the information he or she can. The more knowledge, the greater the confidence and conviction. In human relationships, it's important to get all the information before making any conclusions or judgments. This helps clear up misunderstandings and conflicts.

The same is true spiritually. The more information and facts you know about God, the stronger your understanding and trust in His will for your life.

Faith in God does not make troubles disappear; it makes troubles appear less fearsome because it puts them in the right perspective.

Life Application Bible

Encouragers

Psalm 5:11
Psalm 16:1,2
Psalm 56:3,4

Day 25

Faith

Look at the proud! They trust in themselves, and their lives are crooked; but the righteous will live by their faith (Habakkuk 2:4).

We all live by faith. It is *what* we put our faith in that determines our health and happiness. By faith we drive down the highway expecting others to obey the traffic laws. By faith we eat at restaurants without worrying about being poisoned. And it is by faith that we trust in God through His Son, Jesus. The more we exercise faith, the stronger it becomes in our lives. The more we trust God by faith, the easier it is to trust Him when we don't understand why or what He is doing.

How are you doing in the faith department? Trusting God by faith for the full 42 days will enable you to succeed!

Faith makes the uplook good, the outlook bright, the inlook favorable, and the future glorious.

V. Raymond Edman

Encouragers

Isaiah 26:3
Romans 5:1,2
Hebrews 11:6

Day 26

Patience

God is pleased with you when, for the sake of your conscience, you patiently endure unfair treatment. Of course, you get no credit for being patient if you are beaten for doing wrong. But if you suffer for doing right and are patient beneath the blows, God is pleased with you (1 Peter 2:19,20).

I'm sure you have heard it said, "Lord, give me patience—and I want it now!" Well, have you ever thought about where patience comes from? It comes from trouble. Patience isn't needed when everything is working well and you're getting your way. Patience only increases when it's being exercised. As you persevere through these 42 days, you'll develop more patience because you are working through problems and trials. Patience is an excellent by-product of the process!

One moment of patience may ward off great disaster; one moment of impatience may ruin a whole life.

Author unknown

Encouragers

Proverbs 14:29,30
Ecclesiastes 7:8,9
James 5:7-11

Day 27

Procrastination

Young man, it's wonderful to be young! Enjoy every minute of it. Do everything you want to do; take it all in. But remember that you must give an account to God for everything you do (Ecclesiastes 11:9).

God will judge us for everything we do, including every secret thing, whether good or bad (12:14).

Procrastination involves choosing between two or more courses of action, and people usually end up taking the easiest way out. This is because we want to avoid conflict. Unfortunately, procrastination doesn't erase problems, it only delays our encounter with them. Along with the delay comes worry, anger, and frustration. It's better for the situation and for your health to stop running from responsibility. Make a decision, choose a course of action, and step out in faith to accomplish your goal.

Often we delay doing jobs that seem large, difficult, boring, or disagreeable. But to continue putting them off shows lack of discipline, poor stewardship of time, and in some cases disobedience to God.

Life Application Bible

Encouragers

Proverbs 14:23
Matthew 25:1-13
Hebrews 3:7-19

Day 28

Encouragement

Encourage those who are timid. Take tender care of those who are weak. Be patient with everyone....Always be joyful. Keep on praying. No matter what happens, always be thankful, for this is God's will for you who belong to Christ Jesus (1 Thessalonians 5:14,16-18).

During your journey you have been taking in a lot of information and encouragement. Now it is your turn. Encourage someone today—a family member, a fellow worker, or even a stranger. It is time to turn the focus from yourself to others. It has been said "we only keep what we give away." If you want to be encouraged yourself, start by encouraging others.

Appreciation is thanking, recognition is seeing, and encouragement is bringing hope for the future.

Author unknown

Encouragers

Romans 1:16,17
1 Timothy 4:12-16
1 Peter 1:3-9

Day 29

Trust

You will keep in perfect peace all who trust in you, whose thoughts are fixed on you! Trust in the LORD always, for the LORD GOD is the eternal Rock (Isaiah 26:3,4).

The Bible has a lot to say about trust. I think this repetition is because God knows we wouldn't get it the first time. Humans are so prone to forget God's faithfulness. Sometimes our emotions, past circumstances, and family history get our focus off God. Don't stop the process midstream. Trust God to help you establish new habit patterns. Trust God during this 42-day process.

No matter what may be the test, God will take care of you.
Lean weary one, upon His breast; God will take care of you.

C.D. Martin

Encouragers

Psalm 18:2,3
Psalm 91:1,2
Proverbs 3:5,6

Day 30

Kindness

Since God chose you to be the holy people whom he loves, you must clothe yourselves with tender-hearted mercy, kindness, humility, gentleness, and patience (Colossians 3:12).

It is easy to say something unkind or to do an unkind act. It takes energy, courage, and insight to be thoughtful. You may feel that certain individuals have treated you in a very unkind manner. This hurts. You cannot change what people have done. You can, however, change *your* attitude toward others by being kind to them. Don't follow their poor example. Choose to become known as a very considerate person. You can do it!

The greatness of a man can nearly always be measured by his willingness to be kind.

G. Young

Encouragers

Proverbs 14:21
Galatians 6:9,10
1 Peter 3:8-12

Day 31

Gentleness

But when the Holy Spirit controls our lives, he will produce this kind of fruit in us: love, joy, peace, patience, kindness, goodness, faithfulness, gentleness, and self-control. Here there is no conflict with the law (Galatians 5:22).

When was the last time you consciously thought about being gentle or saying something gentle to others? It is almost impossible to be wrapped up in your own troubles and be gentle at the same time. Gentleness is not a sign of weakness. It is a sign of great strength. As you continue your journey, your focus will change from your own inward struggles to the problems and difficulties others face. When you begin to think of others, your own suffering begins to fade.

If you want happiness for an hour take a nap.
If you want happiness for an day—go fishing.
If you want happiness for an lifetime—help someone else.

Chinese proverb

Encouragers

Isaiah 40:10,11
1 Timothy 6:11
Titus 3:1-8

Day 32

Goodness

Love your enemies! Do good to them! Lend to them! And don't be concerned that they might not repay. Then your reward from heaven will be very great, and you will truly be acting as children of the Most High, for he is kind to the unthankful and to those who are wicked. You must be compassionate, just as your Father is compassionate (Luke 6:35,36).

Our society desperately needs people who display real goodness. The kind that stands for honesty and integrity. William Penn said, "Right is right even if everyone is against it, and wrong is wrong even if everyone is for it." Are you willing to be counted as a person who not only talks goodness, but lives it by helping people who are less fortunate than yourself? Your family will be transformed by goodness if you assume the responsibility for initiating goodness.

Do all the good you can, in all the ways you can, to all the souls you can, in every place you can, at all the times you can, with all the zeal you can, as long as ever you can.

John Wesley

Encouragers

Psalm 119:65,66,68
Proverbs 2:20
Philippians 4:8

Day 33

Love

There are three things that will endure—faith, hope, and love—and the greatest of these is love (1 Corinthians 13:13).

Are you experiencing a broken or damaged relationship? Have you been deeply hurt by someone? How should you respond to these types of circumstances? Act like Jesus would act—and love them! Jesus commanded that we were to love our neighbors as we love ourselves. He then gave us a more difficult command—to love our enemies. This was not a request based on feelings; it is an act of obedience that is stronger than mere emotion. Love people even if they have caused you pain.

Faith, like light, should always be simple and unbending; while love, like warmth, should beam forth on every side and bend to every necessity of our brethren.

Martin Luther

Encouragers

1 Corinthians 13:1-21
Galatians 5:22
1 Peter 1:22

Day 34

Friendship

The heartfelt counsel of a friend is as sweet as perfume and incense (Proverbs 27:9).

Many people complain of not having any friends, and then they just sit around waiting for some to materialize. Here is an age-old principle: To have friends, we must show ourselves friendly. Have you been sitting around waiting for friends to come? Now is the time to get up and get moving. Shakespeare said, "Go oft to the house of your friend for weeds soon choke an unused path." Get out your "weed whacker," and start clearing the path before it becomes too difficult to travel.

Friendship is like a bank account. You can't continue to draw on it without making deposits.

Author unknown

Encouragers

Proverbs 18:24
Proverbs 27:9
Galatians 6:10

Day 35

Service

*Your attitude should be the same that Christ Jesus
had. Though he was God, he did not demand and
cling to his rights as God. He made himself
nothing; he took the humble position of a slave
and appeared in human form* (Philippians 2:5-7).

Throughout history, most of the great heroes are remembered
for how they served others and helped mankind. True happiness does not come from having others wait on us. It comes
from serving others and their needs. When Jesus' disciples
asked Him how to become great in the kingdom of God, He
told them they must become servants. He illustrated this by
becoming a servant Himself and dying for us. With this
example from the King of kings, can we do any less? What
can you do to help someone today?

---

*If you wish to be a leader you will be frustrated,
for very few people wish to be led. If you aim to
be a servant you will never be frustrated.*

Frank F. Warren

Encouragers

Joshua 24:15
Colossians 3:23,24
1 Peter 2:18-20

Day 36

Hope

So I pray that God, who gives you hope, will keep you happy and full of peace as you believe in him. May you overflow with hope through the power of the Holy Spirit (Romans 15:13).

Only six more days to go! I pray that you have been encouraged and reassured by hope that your circumstances are changing or that your attitude in facing them can be more positive and optimistic. One of the greatest gifts we can pass on to others is hope. It is our responsibility and privilege to share how God has helped us grow spiritually. Ask God to lead someone into your life today that you can help support emotionally and strengthen his or her hope for the future.

There is no medicine like hope, no incentive so great, and no tonic so powerful as expectation of something better tomorrow.

Orison Marden

Encouragers

Psalm 38:19
Jeremiah 17:7
Romans 5:1-5

Day 37

Peace

I am leaving you with a gift—peace of mind and heart. And the peace I give isn't like the peace the world gives. So don't be troubled or afraid (John 14:27).

One day a contest was held for artists. They were asked to paint their thoughts about peace. The winner was not the artist who painted a pasture with animals and beautiful sky. It was an artist who painted a raging waterfall. In the midst of the waterfall was an outcropping of rock with a bird on it. It depicted calm peace in the midst of troubled water. God's peace is the same. It comes not when everything is quiet and restful but in the midst of the storms of life. This is the peace that Christ has for you.

---

*Peace is the deliberate adjustment
of my life to the will of God.*

Author unknown

Encouragers

Psalm 4:8
Isaiah 26:3,4
Romans 14:17

Day 38

Joy

*Your words are what sustain me. They bring me
great joy and are my heart's delight, for I bear your
name, O LORD God Almighty* (Jeremiah 15:16).

Where does joy come from? It comes from a true worship of
God and spending time in His presence. It is a gift from the
Holy Spirit of God to those who love and follow the Lord.
Some have suggested that JOY forms an acrostic that stands
for putting Jesus first, Others second, and Yourself last. Have
you made that transition? If not, put Jesus first in all of your
thoughts today. Look for ways to do good to others. Try to
focus on others instead of spending time thinking about your
own problems and difficulties.

---

*Joy is the flag you fly when the Prince of Peace
is in residence within your heart.*

Wilfred Peterson

Encouragers

Psalm 5:11
Psalm 51:8,12
Jude 24

Day 39

Happiness

*How happy are those who fear the L*ORD*—all who follow his ways! You will enjoy the fruit of your labor. How happy you will be! How rich your life!* (Psalm 128:1,2).

Everyone seeks happiness, but somehow it eludes many people. No one can find it directly. It comes only when we busy ourselves in following Christ. Happiness is like the butterfly that is chased but not caught. It is when we stop chasing it that it comes quietly and lands on our shoulder.

If you have been following this 42-day devotional plan and working toward your goals, has happiness snuck up on you yet? My guess is yes!

When one door of happiness closes, another opens, but often we look so long at the closed door that we do not see the one that has been opened for us.

Helen Keller

Encouragers

Psalm 44:15
Proverbs 29:18
Ecclesiastes 5:18-20

Day 40

Thankfulness

Give thanks to the LORD, for he is good! His faithful love endures forever (Psalm 118:1).

In the Old Testament, the Israelites offered many sacrifices to God. The New Testament, however, suggests only one sacrifice. It is found in Hebrews 13:15: "With Jesus' help, let us continually offer our sacrifice of praise to God by proclaiming the glory of his name." One of the secrets to feeling great is learning to be thankful to God for all of His blessings and faithfulness—and that doesn't take 42 days!

A thankful heart is not only the greatest virtue, but the parent of all other virtues.

Cicero

Encouragers

Psalm 13:6
Psalm 28:7
Psalm 40:1-5

Day 41

Will of God

Don't copy the behavior and customs of this world, but let God transform you into a new person by changing the way you think. Then you will know what God wants you to do, and you will know how good and pleasing and perfect his will really is (Romans 12:2).

Finding the will of God is not a big mystery. We do not have to look very far. All we have to do is open the Bible and seek God. He will give us peace, joy, and happiness—and reveal what His will is for us.

You are close to completing your 42 days. Keep seeking to know God more intimately. His desire is to draw you to Himself and give you great comfort. He who began a good work in you will continue to perform it until you meet Him face to face. That is exciting news!

---

*To know the will of God is the highest of all wisdom.
You can be happy in the midst of suffering if you are
in God's will.... You can be calm and at peace in the midst
of persecution, as long as you are in the will of God.*

Billy Graham

Encouragers

1 Thessalonians 4:3
1 Thessalonians 5:18
Hebrews 13:20,21

Day 42

Word of God

All Scripture is inspired by God and is useful to teach us what is true and to make us realize what is wrong in our lives. It straightens us out and teaches us to do what is right. It is God's way of preparing us in every way, fully equipped for every good thing God wants us to do (2 Timothy 3:16,17).

You made it! Congratulations! The Word of God has influenced your thinking. It is God's Word that has given you encouragement and direction. Do not stop on this last day of your journey to feeling great. Keep discovering all that God has for you. Abraham Lincoln said, "In regard to this great Book [the Bible], I have but to say, it is the best gift God has given man. All the good the Savior gave to the world was communicated through this book. But for it we could not know right from wrong."

It ain't those parts of the Bible that I can't understand that bother me, it is the parts that I do understand.

Mark Twain

The Bible will keep you from sin, or sin will keep you from the Bible.

D. L. Moody

Encouragers

Joshua 1:8
Psalm 119:9-11
Jeremiah 15:16

12 Steps for Christian Living

1. We admit our need for God's gift of salvation, that we are powerless over certain areas of our lives and that our lives are at times sinful and unmanageable.

2. We come to believe through the Holy Spirit that a power who came in the person of Jesus Christ and who is greater than ourselves can transform our weaknesses into strengths.

3. We make a decision to turn our will and our lives over to the care of Jesus Christ as we understand Him—hoping to understand Him more fully.

4. We make a searching and fearless moral inventory of ourselves—both our strengths and our weaknesses.

5. We admit to Christ, to ourselves, and to another human being the exact nature of our sins.

6. We become entirely ready to have Christ heal all of these defects of character that prevent us from having a more spiritual lifestyle.

7. We humbly ask Christ to transform all of our shortcomings.

8. We make a list of all persons we have harmed and become willing to make amends to them all.

9. We make direct amends to such persons whenever possible, except when to do so would injure them or others.

10. We continue to take personal inventory and when we are wrong, promptly admit it, and when we are right, thank God for His guidance.

11. We seek through prayer and meditation to improve our conscious contact with Jesus Christ as we understand Him, praying for knowledge of His will for us and the power to carry that out.

12. Having experienced a new sense of spirituality as a result of these steps and realizing that this is a gift of God's grace, we are willing to share the message of His love and forgiveness with others and to practice these principles for spiritual living in all our affairs.*

I agree with these 12 steps:

Signed_____

Date _____

---

* Rev. Vernon Bittner, "12–Steps for Christian Living," Institute for Christian Living, Minnetrista, MN, 55364–7713. Used by permission

Help from the Bible

Abortion

Jeremiah 1:1-5
Psalm 139:1-24
2 Chronicles 28:1-8

Abusive Behavior

Romans 12:10
Romans 12:18,19
1 Corinthians 10:31
1 Thessalonians 5:15
James 1:20

Accountability

Joshua 7:1-15
Judges 6:1-16
Ecclesiastes 12:13,14
Romans 14:1-22

Adultery

Isaiah 1
Hosea 1
Matthew 5:27-32
Luke 16:16-18
John 8:1-11

Advice

Proverbs 1:1-9
Proverbs 6:20-24
Proverbs 10:1-21
Mark 10:17-31

Affections

Proverbs 4:23-27

Alcoholism

Proverbs 20:1
Proverbs 23:29-35
1 Corinthians 15:33
2 Peter 2:19

Anger

Matthew 5:21-26
Ephesians 4:26-32
James 3:6

Anxiety

Psalm 16:11
Psalm 37:1,7
Proverbs 16:7
Isaiah 41:10

Arguments

Proverbs 15:1-9
Proverbs 26:17-28
Philippians 2:12-18
Titus 3:1-11

Attitude

Philippians 2:5-11
Philippians 4:4-9

Backsliding

Deuteronomy 8:10-20
Luke 9:57-62
James 5:15-20

Belief

Romans 10:5-13
James 2:14-24

Bereavement
Deuteronomy 31:8
Psalm 23:1-6
Psalm 27:10
Psalm 119:50

Bitterness
Hebrews 12:14-17
1 John 3:11-24

Choices
Proverbs 1
Proverbs 13:1-16
Matthew 9:9-13

Comfort
Job 16
Lamentations 3:21-26
2 Corinthians 1:3-11

Complaining
Philippians 2:12-18

Confidence
Matthew 10:26-42
Acts 5:17-26

Conflicts
James 4:1-12

Conscience
Proverbs 28:13-18
Acts 23:1
Acts 24:16
1 Timothy 3:8,9
Hebrews 10:21,22
1 Peter 3:16

Criticism
Matthew 7:1-5

Deceit
Exodus 20:1-21

Depression
1 Kings 19:1-9
Psalm 42

Desires
Psalm 97

Despair
Exodus 14:1-14
Psalm 40

Difficulties
Romans 8:28
2 Corinthians 4:17
Hebrews 12:7-11
Revelation 3:19

Disappointment
Psalm 43:5
Psalm 55:22
Psalm 126:6
John 14:27
2 Corinthians 4:8-10

Discouragement
Joshua 1:9
Psalm 27:14
Colossians 1:5
1 Peter 1:3-9
1 John 5:14

Discernment
Matthew 7:1-12
James 1:2-8

Luke 17:1-10
Galatians 5:13-26

Dishonesty

Proverbs 20:23-30

Disobedience

Genesis 3
1 Chronicles 13

Divisions

1 Corinthians 4:6-13

Divorce and Remarriage

Malachi 2:15,16
Matthew 19:8,9
1 Corinthians 7:10-15

Drinking

Proverbs 23:29-35
Ephesians 5:15-20

Encouragement

1 Thessalonians 5
1 Peter 1:1-13

Enthusiasm

Colossians 3:18-25

Envy

Deuteronomy 5:21
1 Kings 21

Eternal Life

Luke 18:18-30
John 3:1-21
John 6:60-71
John 17
1 John 5:1-13

Faults

Matthew 7:1-5
Ephesians 4:1-16

Fear

Joshua 1
Psalm 27:1
Psalm 56:11
Psalm 91:1-6
Psalm 121
Proverbs 29:25

Feelings

Romans 5:9-21

Foolishness

Psalm 14
Proverbs 9
1 Corinthians 2:6-16

Forgiveness

Psalm 51
Matthew 6:5-15
Matthew 18:21-35
Romans 12
1 John 1

Friendship

Proverbs 17
John 15:1-17

Frustration

Ephesians 6:1-4

Gambling

Proverbs 15:16
Proverbs 23:4,5
Luke 12:15
1 Timothy 6:9

Gentleness

2 Timothy 2:14-26
James 3:1-18

Gossip
Exodus 23:1-9
Proverbs 25:18-28
2 Thessalonians 3:6-15

Greed
James 4

Guilt
Psalm 32:1,2
Romans 8:1-17
Colossians 2:9-17
1 John 3:11-24

Habits
1 John 3

Happiness
Matthew 5:1-12
1 Timothy 6:3-10

Heaven
John 14:1-14
Colossians 3:1-17

Hell
Matthew 25:41-46
Romans 1:18-32
Revelation 20:1-15

Help
Psalm 46
Galatians 6:1-10

Homosexuality
Romans 1:18-32
1 Corinthians 6:9-11
1 Timothy 1:1-11

Hope
Romans 5:1-11
1 Thessalonians 4:13-18

Hurt
Psalm 55:22
Psalm 56:3,4
Psalm 121
1 Peter 5:7

Immorality
1 Corinthians 6
Revelation 9:13-21

Indecisiveness
John 3:22-36

Inferiority
Psalm 63:3
Psalm 86:13
Psalm 139:13-16
1 Corinthians 1:26-29
1 Peter 2:9,10

Insult
Proverbs 12

Integrity
Psalm 25
Luke 16:1-15

Jealousy
Romans 13

Judging
Matthew 7:1-6
1 Corinthians 5:1-13

Kindness
Luke 6:27-36
Colossians 3:1-17

Laziness
2 Thessalonians 3:6-15
2 Peter 3:1-18

Lifestyle
Matthew 5:1-12
1 Corinthians 9
2 Timothy 2:14-26

Loneliness
Psalm 23
Isaiah 41:10
Matthew 28:20
Hebrews 13:5,6

Lust
Mark 7:20-23
Romans 6:12
1 Thessalonians 4:3-8
James 1:14,15

Lying
Proverbs 17:20
Proverbs 19:9
Proverbs 24:24
Proverbs 26:28
Proverbs 29:12
Matthew 5:37
Ephesians 4:17-32

Materialism
Matthew 6:19 24

Morality
Romans 2:1-16
Romans 12:1-8

Motives
Jeremiah 17:1-18
James 4:1-12

Murder
Deuteronomy 5:1-33
James 5:1-6

Obedience
Deuteronomy 30:11-19
Romans 5

Occult
Deuteronomy 18:9-13
1 Samuel 28:7-12
2 Kings 21:6
Isaiah 47:13,14
Acts 19:18-20

Pain
Hebrews 12:1-13

Peace
Psalm 3
John 14
Romans 5:1-11

Priorities
Proverbs 3
Matthew 6:25-34

Problems
James 1:1-18

Procrastination
Proverbs 10
Proverbs 26

Quarrels
Proverbs 13:1-10
Titus 3:1-11
James 4:1-12

Relationships
2 Corinthians 6:14-18
Ephesians 2:11-22

Resentment
James 1

Revenge
Romans 12:17-21

Righteousness
Psalm 51
2 Corinthians 5:11-21

Self-Centeredness
Mark 8:31-38
1 Peter 1:14-25

Selfishness
Mark 8:31-38
James 4:1-10

Sex
Proverbs 5:15-21
1 Corinthians 7:1-11
1 Thessalonians 4:1-8

Sickness
Psalm 41:3
Psalm 103:3
Matthew 4:23
John 11:4
James 5:13-15

Sin
Isaiah 53:5,6
Isaiah 59:1,2
John 8:34
Romans 3:23
Romans 6:23
Galatians 6:7,8

Stress
Romans 5:1-5
Philippians 4:4-9

Suffering
Romans 8:18
2 Corinthians 1:5
Philippians 3:10
2 Timothy 2:12
James 1:2-8
1 Peter 1:6,7

Suicide
Job 14:5
Romans 14:7
1 Corinthians 6:19,20
James 4:7

Temptation
Psalm 94:17,18
Proverbs 28:13
1 Corinthians 10:12,13
Hebrews 4:14-16
James 1:2-14

Terminal Illness
Jeremiah 29:11
2 Corinthians 12:9
1 Thessalonians 5:18
2 Timothy 2:12

Thankfulness
Psalm 92
Romans 1:18-23
Ephesians 2:1-10

Unpardonable Sin
Matthew 12:31,32
Mark 3:28,29

Waiting
Psalm 27
Psalm 40:1-4
Matthew 24:32-51

Weakness

2 Corinthians 12:1-10
1 John 3:1-11

Will of God

Psalm 37:4
Psalm 91:1,2
Proverbs 3:5,6
Proverbs 4:26
Romans 14:5
Galatians 6:4
Ephesians 5:15-21
Philippians 2:12,13
1 Thessalonians 4:3
1 Peter 3:17

Wisdom

Psalm 119:97-112
Proverbs 1:1-7
Ecclesiastes 8:1-8
Luke 2:33-40
James 1:2-8

Worry

Psalm 37:1-11
Matthew 6:25-34
Philippians 4:4-9

Is it possible to live life
without a purpose...

Lonely, Frustrated, & Unhappy

The rise in divorce, mental and emotional breakdowns, crime, suicide, and the unhappiness of many indicate that it's impossible.

Is it possible to experience
joy, peace, and happiness,
and to have a

Dynamic living is only found in a personal relationship with God... made possible by Jesus Christ.

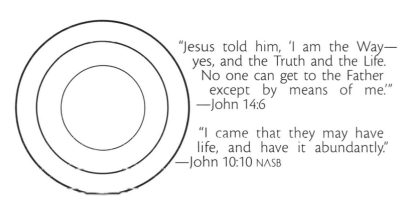

"Jesus told him, 'I am the Way—yes, and the Truth and the Life. No one can get to the Father except by means of me.'"
—John 14:6

"I came that they may have life, and have it abundantly."
—John 10:10 NASB

To understand this concept, let's take a look at man's beginning in the Garden of Eden.

God created man in His own image.

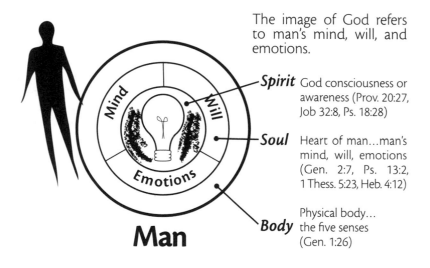

The image of God refers to man's mind, will, and emotions.

Spirit God consciousness or awareness (Prov. 20:27, Job 32:8, Ps. 18:28)

Soul Heart of man...man's mind, will, emotions (Gen. 2:7, Ps. 13:2, 1 Thess. 5:23, Heb. 4:12)

Body Physical body... the five senses (Gen. 1:26)

Man

In the beginning God and man had perfect fellowship (relationship).

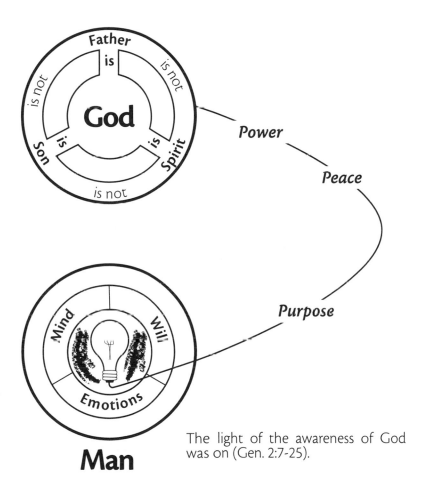

The light of the awareness of God was on (Gen. 2:7-25).

Man disobeyed and his relationship with God was broken.

See Gen. 2:17, 3:1-24

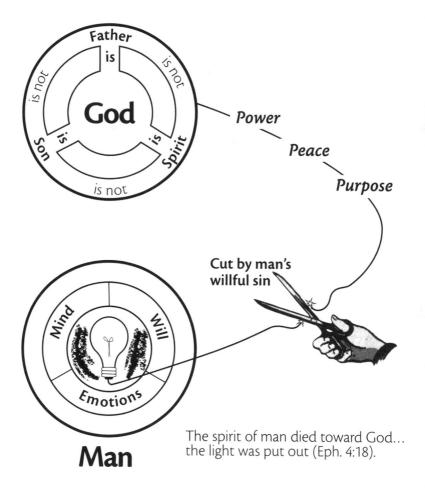

Father
is
is not
is not
God
Son
is
is
Spirit
is not

Power

Peace

Purpose

Cut by man's
willful sin

Mind
Will
Emotions

Man

The spirit of man died toward God...
the light was put out (Eph. 4:18).

God does not force us to love Him... the choice is ours.

Man

Man chose to disobey God. This disobedience was sin.

"When Adam sinned, sin entered the entire human race. His sin spread death throughout all the world, so everything began to grow old and die, for all sinned" (Rom. 5:12).

"For all have sinned and fall short of the glory of God" (Rom. 3:23 NIV).

The wages of sin is death.
Death is eternal separation from God

Rom. 6:23

What is the remedy?

Jesus is the only way back to God.

John 14:6

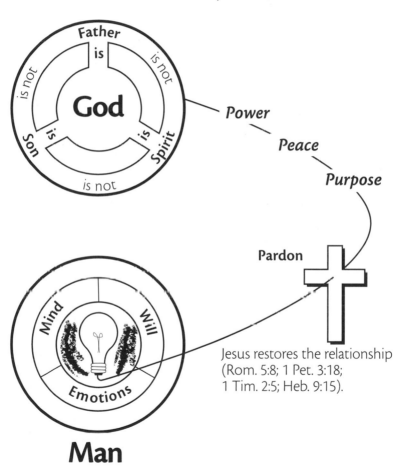

Power

Peace

Purpose

Pardon

Jesus restores the relationship
(Rom. 5:8; 1 Pet. 3:18;
1 Tim. 2:5; Heb. 9:15).

Man

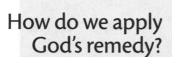

How do we apply
God's remedy?

Receive Jesus into your heart by faith.

"But to all who receive him he gave the
right to become children of God. All
they needed to do was to trust him to
save them."
John 1:12

Free gift
(Rom. 6:23,
Eph. 2:8-9)

What happens when one receives Jesus into his life?

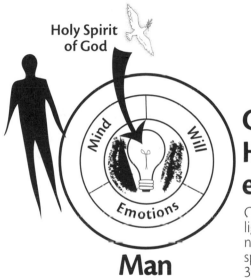

God by His Holy Spirit enters our life.

God again turns on the light of God consciousness or awareness in the spirit of man (see Titus 3:5,6).

Would you like to experience a dynamic life? Would you like to receive Jesus?

You can by a simple prayer of faith. Remember that becoming a Christian is not just saying words... it's receiving a person—*Jesus.*

Dear Lord Jesus:
I would like to receive You into my life.
Thank You for dying in my place. Thank
You for pardoning my sins. Thank You
for the gift of eternal life. Help me, by
Your Holy Spirit, to live for You.
Amen.

"When someone becomes a Christian, he becomes a brand-new person inside. He is not the same anymore. A new life has begun!"

2 Cor. 5:17

To help you in this dynamic life...Jesus must be the controller of your life.

Jesus wants to reinvade your mind, will, and emotions and establish His control.

To help you grow in the Christian life remember to...

1. Thank God for your new relationship with Him.
   Rev. 3:20, Col. 1:14,27; 1 John 5:11-13, John 6:37, Rom. 10:9-13, Heb. 13:5

2. Read God's Word daily.
   1 Peter 2:2, Psalm 119:9,11

3. Talk to God and keep your sins confessed up to date.
   1 John 1:9, Ps. 66:18, Phil. 4:6-7

4. Fellowship with other believers...fellowship in a church where Christ is preached.
   Heb. 10:25

5. Tell others about Jesus.
   Mark 5:19, Matt. 28:19-20, Acts 1:8

More Books by
Bob Phillips

Anger Is a Choice
Awesome Good Clean Jokes for Kids
Bob Phillips' Encyclopedia of Good Clean Jokes
A Classic Collection of Golf Jokes & Quotes
Controlling Your Emotions Before They Control You
The Delicate Art of Dancing with Porcupines
Extremely Good Clean Jokes for Kids
How Can I Be Sure?—Questions to Ask Before You Get Married
Humor Is Tremendous
In Search of Bible Trivia
Over the Hill & On a Roll
Phillips' Awesome Collection of Quips & Quotes
Phillips' Book of Great Thoughts & Funny Sayings
Super-Duper Good Clean Jokes for Kids
The World's Greatest Collection of Clean Jokes
The World's Greatest Knock-Knock Jokes for Kids

For more information on books by Bob Phillips or to purchase any of the above books, please contact your local Christian bookstore or send a self-addressed stamped envelope to:

Family Services
PO Box 9363
Fresno, CA 93763

Also by Bob Phillips...

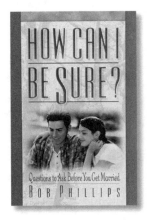

How Can I Be Sure?

For more than 20 years this premarriage inventory has helped couples contemplating marriage. Readers explore their thoughts and feelings, find areas of agreement, and develop a basis for resolving disagreements.

Over the Hill & On a Roll

You will enjoy laughing at insights, testing your memory, and taking history quizzes created by jokester Bob Phillips. Packed with wisdom and fascinating facts, *Over the Hill & On a Roll* celebrates the passing of time and pokes fun at what lies ahead.

Also by Bob Phillips...

Controlling Your Emotions Before They Control You

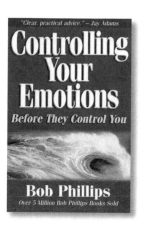

The roller-coaster ride of emotional turmoil can be devastating. Fear, anger, and stress take their toll, and families are hurt, job performance suffers, and self-esteem plummets. Is there hope? In this hands-on guide, readers will find practical help in:

- dealing with depression
- overcoming bitterness
- understanding feelings
- forgiving others
- praising God in the midst of problems

True stories, emotional evaluations, personality charts, and biblical counsel make this book understandable and interesting.